LEADERSHIP TIME TO TURN THE PAGE

Learn How to Become a Transformational Leader Starting Today

PART-II

Tracy G. Jilge-Holzberlein

Copyright @ 2022

Self-Published by Kindle Direct Publishing

All rights reserved. No part of this publication may be reproduced, stored in a retrieval system, or transmitted, in any form or by any means, electronic, mechanical, photocopying, recording, or otherwise, without the prior written permission of the publisher.

ISBN: 9798367279825

This book is dedicated to:

The women along my way who made an impact on my life: Linda J. Watts, Barbara Brown, Terry Carter, Kim Brown, Tammy Gorman, Gail Cassity, Ashlan Rose Gilfedder, and Tammy Fredrick. It is not always the big moments in life that you remember and make an impact on you. It is the little things along the way that build a strong foundation that is unbreakable.

Linda Jean Watts: A beautiful soul, inside and out. Although, you are gone, you will never be forgotten. You gave your heart and soul to everyone you met. You taught me life is too short to stay a wallflower. Life is way more fun when you put your feet into the soil and feel the earth move. You were always there for me in times of darkness. But It is the good times we shared that stand out in my heart the most. You taught me how to dance to the music in my soul. I will forever, be grateful.

Barbara Brown: Another beautiful soul to cross my path. Every person you meet is for a reason, a season, or a lifetime. You are my lifetime friend. We can be apart for years and when we meet back up, the smiles and laughs are on. We have been friends since our sons were in grade school. I can always count on you to brighten my world. I love you and I am so grateful for you.

Terry Carter: It is hard to put into words how I feel about you, my soul sister. We have been friends since sixth grade (forty-eight years). You and your family loved my brother John and I as if we belonged to you. You have the strongest character and biggest heart of anyone I know. Even during hard times of your life, you made room for me. You taught me life is not about material things, but the bond that is forged through love and friendship. May it always be this way, in the world.

Kim Brown: Another forty-eight-year friendship. I love you to the moon and back. You speak right to my heart. I will always remember singing "Moon River" with you at the local Yell County Talent Show. Despite my brother and his pals cackling in the back of the room, your vocals were natural talent, and I was in awe. I still am. Soul sisters forever.

Tammy Gorman: Forty-eight years seems like yesterday. You are another soul sister to me. You taught me about faith. You have the strongest faith of anyone I know. You were raised by a strong woman of faith and had a wonderful father. I loved growing up in Yell County, Arkansas. Horses, farms, hard work, good country cooking, and God, changed my life. You inspire me every single day. I love you to the moon and back. You taught me to hold on strong. It is the only way. You only must Believe. I love you girl.

Gail Cassity: Forty-eight-year friendships seem to be the norm when it comes to Yell County, Arkansas. You have taught me so much about life. You shared great times with me like the Yell County Fair, snipe hunting during a full moon, and my first taste of real strawberry wine. We have had a lot of fun over the years, never to be forgotten. Our bond is strong and will last forever. I love you to the moon and back.

Ashlan Rose Gilfedder: My truly most beautiful and only niece. You have taught me more than anyone I know. You are the most amazing woman, and you are going to be the same, most amazing mother soon. I am so proud of you and all you have accomplished on your own. You inspire me every single day to be a better version of myself. I just need to hang out for a single afternoon, and I can make a whole list of things I want to do better, to be more at peace, and in alignment with my true purpose in this life, like you are doing. I love you kiddo.

Tammy Fredrick: My dearest cousin. I am so thankful we have had the time to share over the years, traveling all over the place, bringing us closer. You bring laughter and smiles to this old girl's face. It is difficult to pick my favorite, most memorable, of all trips, but I think it boils down to the remote northern high Sierra mountains. Trout fishing, gold panning, and a surprise visit by a wayward Folsom prison road crew worker, naked as a jail bird. The word "RUN" took an all-new meaning. It is a wonder we are still alive. I love you girl.

Preface

When I think of leadership, I think of the road I have traveled to get here. It is the strong bonds I have forged along the way that have built the layers of strength it takes to be a leader. It is not about titles, along the way. It is not about money. It is about the heart and what it is capable of. It is about setting boundaries, not walls, to allow people in. It is about the people you meet along the way that have something you need to learn, or something you need to share with them. When I share my life experiences, they are my life experiences. They are not up for debate. The opinion of others does not matter to me and is not important. I am sharing my life experiences in the hope it will help someone else down the road, to learn and grow.

It is about failures. When you come from nothing, then every experience is either a win or a lesson. I will share many failures from my life experience. Every failure I have had was a tiny setback compared to the big comebacks, failing forward. It can be exciting to learn so much and feel the growth of your own soul. When you focus on growing into the best person you were always meant to be, you do not have time to care or give a flip about people who want to see you fail. Believe me, everyone has people like that in their lives. Those are the shallow, toxic, evil, and self-centered people who will exhaust all efforts to keep the light from shining on them. In the end, time and the truth will hold them accountable. Wish them well, walk away, and live the life meant for you.

This book is Part II of Leadership – Time to Turn the Page. I will be talking a lot about primary foods. As a certified International Integrative Nutrition Health Coach, I will share with you how primary foods are not necessarily food, but things that feed your soul. Things that help you live a very fulfilled and joyful life. The main primary foods I will talk about will be listed as the seven main dimensions of the whole person. There are many more dimensions that make up a whole person and I will be talking about those as well. As a leader, it is important you analyze yourself in these wellness dimensions. When you are in balance, then you can be a perfect role model to lead your organization into a more holistic style of leadership.

In 2012, Americans spent 30.2 billion dollars out of pocket on complimentary health approaches. (NCCIH, NIH.gov, 2022). That was ten years ago. Complimentary health approaches:

include Ayurveda, biofeedback, chelation therapy, chiropractic or osteopathic manipulation, craniosacral therapy, energy healing therapy, guided imagery, herbs and other non-vitamin supplements, hypnosis, homeopathy, massage, acupuncture, meditation (mantra, mindfulness, and spiritual), Reiki, breath work, functional food therapy, and even essential oil therapy. Complimentary methods are also called integrative methods. 1.9 billion dollars was spent on children's wellness. People are searching for wellness. People are searching for wholeness and for what is missing in their lives. I am going to be talking a lot about this.

The world is evolving into a more holistic way of life, in all areas. In order for a person to be completely balanced, all areas of the person's life need to be recognized and attentive to. It is so easy to focus on only one thing, such as, career. However, that is not a healthy way to be. It is very difficult to do, believe me. I am still a work in progress. As corporations move in the direction of holistic leadership, it is important to keep in mind, you are important, also. You have the power to create positive change within your organization. Many organizations are creating unique wellness in the workplace centers that inspire everyone. It is a great opportunity for leaders to become involved from the ground up.

As with my first book, this work is directly inspired from my personal life experiences. Most people are too afraid to share their stories, for fear of rejection, humiliation, or shame. It is our stories that can inspire others to keep their chin up, to keep plugging away at those dreams, to keep our hearts soft and open to new experiences and relationships. To live a life filled with love and peace takes a lot of hard work, forgiveness, and sacrifice. The most important thing to remember is everyone is capable of growth. Growth of the human spirit is a beautiful thing. Growth can be a painful lifelong process, but in the end, it can be very rewarding.

I am nobody famous or special. Life is hard for us all. There is not much that I cannot relate to. I am certain you will find something you can relate to also upon reading this book. I come from the humblest of beginnings, growing up in the poorest of environments. I have been dirt poor, and I have been very comfortable throughout my life, experiencing both ends of the spectrum.

One thing I do know from my life is that every road we take does lead somewhere. It leads to choices we have to make. In my life, I have made good choices and I have made bad choices. All the choices I have made have taught me hard life lessons. But each life experience has inspired me to keep moving forward to become a better person than I was the day before. If I could not find a way to keep myself from falling backwards, I made a different choice. I made a conscious choice to move forward, and I chose the best option to do so. It was not always the choice others thought I should make, but it was mine.

When other people cannot control you, then they try to control how other people see you. This usually involves a false narrative of some sort. You cannot control what other people say. You cannot control other people's opinions. In the end, their opinions are not important. Their opinions do not define who you are. Their opinions do not matter. These people do not matter. It is important you keep hold of your own reins to your life. Even if that means, walking away. This can be applied to relationships as much as it can be applied to professional careers. The minute you are disrespected and feel you must prove your worth to someone, is the absolute minute to walk away.

This book is also about communication, diversity, mindfulness, and gratitude. I start my day, every single day, taking five minutes to write down everything I am grateful for, in that moment. I also set the tone for what I hope to accomplish that day. At the end of the day, I write down my highlights of the day. They can be very simple and not even relate to work. It is the strength of the relationships we create that sustain us through the everyday life. My niece gave me a book called, "The Five-Minute Journal". It is awesome. It has been interesting to see how my gratitude has changed, in only a few days. I am worth more than five minutes a day. So are you. It is a great way to get focused on a holistic way (outside of your day planner).

Back in the early nineteen-eighties, I wrote an essay on Sigmund Freud. I not only made an A on the paper but received extra points. My professor asked if she could distribute my work at a psychology conference. Of course, I said yes. I recently read a quote of Freud's that said, "Unexpressed emotions never die, they are buried alive, and come forth in the ugliest of ways, down the road". I remember reading this forty years ago. It is very true. I will talk about unexpressed emotions in this book and how it can relate to leadership down the road.

This book is also about personal relationships. If you are not happy at home, it bleeds into your everyday work life. A lot of times, we end up taking things out on the people who work for us, without realizing it. Also, if we are not happy at work, we go home and take it out on the people we truly love and care about.

Relationships are not easy. Life is too short to be unhappy, or sad. It takes a tremendous amount of courage to initiate change, especially, in personal relationships. I want to say, the older you are, the harder it is. But I would be wrong. It is damn hard, at any age. The decision to change is the hard part. Once, you make that choice, the rest falls right into place. I will say, also, you can love someone for years and reach a point where you realize, you cannot live with them any longer. It doesn't have to be a love/hate relationship. The important thing to remember, is that you matter. Your life is important, too. We get so busy putting everyone before ourselves, we lose ourselves. Some might say, well, this is about being selfless. I say, you cannot pour from an empty cup. You must put yourself first. That is the most selfless thing you can do, for you. It is all about balance. If you take a good hard look at your life and see it is unbalanced in any area, take the time to fix it. Or at least, take small baby steps towards change.

It could be work causing the unhappiness. I know it is scary to walk away from a paycheck. But your health is more important. High stress leads to strokes, heart attacks, and even cancer. When I had my first bout of cancer in 1986, (at age 24), the first thing my physician told me was, "you have to get rid of everything that is causing you stress, whether it is a marriage, a job, or any other relationship". This was the best advice anyone could ever give.

To become a transformational leader, you must first handle your own emotions, relationships, and stress. It takes a very high emotional intelligence to put others above your own needs. If you are personally struggling with issues from the past, you must understand your own feelings and emotions, deal with them, and put them aside, before you can reach other people and become a leader of transformation in your organization.

Every choice I have made in my life, from growing up in rural Arkansas's Ouachita and Ozark mountains, to picking up everything and moving to rural Alaska, and returning home to Oklahoma, has brought challenges and life changes that only propelled me forward. Sometimes, I could not see the forest for the many trees in my path. Sometimes, it takes poor choices mixed with good choices, life lessons, and heartbreak to become the person you were truly meant to be. Life has a way of humbling you and reminding you of what is most important.

We are living in a different time than ever before. The only thing I am certain of is change. It is constant. As we migrate through global viruses, political wars, turmoil everywhere we live and work, I see executive leadership changing, relationships changing, workforce environments changing. The following pages of this book are guides to how we need to evolve as a global society to survive. Embracing change is the only way through this mud and muck we find ourselves currently in.

In this Part II book, I will dive deeper into a lot of topics. As with anything, you can apply it, or not. This is my story. I own it. My only hope is to inspire, laugh, empower, and create positive change. Even if it is only one person. As with Part I, I have combined my personal experiences with my Capstone research project and all references are cited in the back of the book. I hope you enjoy Part II as much as I enjoyed writing it.

Prologue

Everything we do is about the past, present, and future. As a society, we have learned a lot. Look around and see how much growth we have. Look around and see how far we have come. We truly are living on the edge of change. History is who we are. We have the power to change the course of the entire world and become a true leader of holistic transformational leadership. It is true that history shapes leadership. It is also true that leadership is defiant of history because of the continual progression of the world and business.

Research and studies continue to search for the best leadership practices around the world, even as the world is changing. Whether the lessons learned from Nelson Mandela, or the queens and kings of centuries past have become guidelines to adhere by, the truth of the matter is, great leaders share where they have been and who they are. They can step outside of themselves for a moment in time to create and share a vision of where they are headed and engage the support of followers.

These great leaders transform the very word leadership, by the way they build relationships based on trust and respect. They take time to develop talent in the people who serve the organizations. They have strong ethics and moral cores that become role models for others to follow. These leaders care about people and put people first, above their own needs and desires. These great leaders transform organizations by supporting healthy environments, healthy employees, and healthy cultures.

This guidebook demonstrates how important it is to look and support the whole person. In this way, leaders will become transformational and create organizations that are stronger and better than any other time in history.

The topic of leadership has evolved over many centuries. Hundreds of researchers have spent countless hours searching for the best practices of leadership. As with everything, leadership is constantly changing. The world is constantly changing. Business is constantly changing. The workforce is constantly changing. These things alone require new ways of doing business and new ways of managing human capital.

As the world evolves, leadership is moving towards a more holistic style that puts people first. This book will dive into the different dimensions of the whole person and how it relates to leadership. The overall wellness of the people employed in organizations has proven how important it is for productivity, profitability, employee satisfaction, and sustainability. It is time for leaders to evolve into the next future type of leader.

This book will demonstrate what best practices are needed to build a strong sustainable organizational environment and why they are needed in this time of global movement and change management. Leadership is changing from people serving organizations to leadership serving the people. Leadership has entered a time when they are becoming teachers of excellence. It sounds great. I love the word "excellence". Who would not want to be part of that?

Great leaders take the time to build relationships through trust and respect. In this way, they become transformational in the organization. Great leaders share their stories. They share where they have been and who they are. They step outside of themselves for a moment in time to create and share a vision of where they are headed and engage the support of followers. Great leaders are leaders who take care of themselves, find a solid balance between work and life, are relaxed and willing to share their knowledge with their people to ensure they keep growing. Great leaders are humble, respectful, and have a high level of integrity. They walk their talk.

With globalization, many corporations have expanded around the world. This is great. I will also be talking about expatriates and repatriation programs. There is so much to learn and so much needed to create wellness environments for the employees who accept these difficult assignments out of the country. Expatriates experience a whole different dimension of health risks, safety issues, and even different performance appraisals or reviews.

As you read this book, it does not matter what level of leader you are, or even if you are a leader. I want you to think about what kind of legacy you are going to leave behind when you are gone. We are all just humans living on this earth for a short time. Everywhere you look, people are hurting. They are hurting in a million different ways. It is how we open our hearts and love on people, no matter where they are in life, that will leave a mark. It is in your power to leave a good one. We are entering a great movement towards holistic leadership. We need to be on the forefront of that movement.

Table of Contents

1. Introduction
2. The Whole Person-Career/Occupational
3. The Whole Person-Spirituality
4. The Whole Person-Financial
5. The Whole Person-Family/Environmental
6. The Whole Person-Social
7. The Whole Person-Creativity/Intellectual
8. The Whole Person-Health/Physical
9. Talent Segmentation – Staffing
10. The True Value of Human Resources
11. Human Resources and Job Descriptions
12. Human Resource Challenges
13. Human Resources Training & Development
14. Best Practices for International Human Resources
15. Primary Aspects of International Human Resources
16. Expatriate Recruitment
17. Build or Buy Talent
18. Compensation/Performance Reviews
19. Mental Health in the Workplace
20. Ethical Exit Surveys
21. Organizational Economics
22. Importance of Analyzing Risks in Business

23. Strategic Improvements for Business Meetings
24. Managerial Strategies for Interview Communications
25. Best Managerial Communication Tools
26. IT for Managers
27. Best Communication Skills for Business
28. Leadership Writing Skills and How it Can Affect Morale
29. Emotional Intelligence for Advanced Levels
30. Nonverbal Communication Skills
31. Fostering a Listening Climate
32. Cultural Communications
33. Conflict Resolution Skills for Managers
34. Don't Be a Groupthink
35. Management Communications Systems
36. Gender Communications
37. Reiki/Tai Chi/Qi Gong/Yoga
38. Reflexology
39. Massage Therapy
40. Functional Food
41. Global Wellness/PTSD/Trauma
42. Energy Psychology/Tapping
43. Wellness Checks
44. Meditation
45. Culture

46. Diversity

47. Mindfulness

48. Gratitude

49. Fear

50. Detox & Cleanse

51. Whole Food Nutrition

52. Kindness

53. Integrity

54. Understanding Change

55. The Heart & Love

56. Recap

57. Conclusion

Unplugged Part II

Fear, Folly, and Failure

There were only two places in the world I felt safe when I was growing up. The first place was a two-foot crawl space above our chicken coop that was filled with pigeon poop and fiddle back spiders. The other place was at the top of the biggest Mimosa tree I have ever seen, perched between a solid strand of limbs and a soft goose down feather pillow. I might add, I usually had a Harlequin Romance novel with me, to kill the time. I always thought to myself, better to kill the time, out of sight, than for me to be within range of abuse inside the house.

There was something soothing about the smell of the soft feathery pink flowers of the Mimosa tree. In the fall, sometimes, I would spend hours picking the brown mimosa seeds and running a needle through the middle of them to make a necklace. The important thing was, it was so high up, nobody ever looked for me there. I could watch from above, as my name was called, over and over. The old saying "kids are to be seen and not heard", was my daily motto. This was not because it was beaten into us every single day, but because it was the only smart thing left to do. Only, in my mind, the best part of that, was to be NOT seen, and NOT heard.

There were times when I hid from sunup to sundown in the crawl space of the chicken coop. We never had much food. I was very disciplined in the way I could make a box of dry orange jello last a whole day. We always had boxes of jello in the cupboard, along with a tin of powdered eggs and cans of spam. Back in the early sixties and seventies, the government handed out food once a month to people who were struggling to find ways to feed their families. Every month, we would go with my mother and stand in the long line, just to get a box of powdered eggs, spam, and a few other staples, like beans. When my grandpa Claude was alive, it seemed we always had plenty of fresh pork, fresh beef, fresh catfish, and fresh eggs. But he died when I was twelve.

My stepdad would not even let my mother go to her own father's funeral. He said it was because he was not a Jehovah's Witness. But I know that was not true, because he allowed me to go. I will never forget the day when my mom and stepfather fought about that. My mother was yelling at my stepfather, and he reached out and put his hands around her throat, choking her until she passed out. My brother Johnnie, jumped on his back and began beating my stepfather in the head with his fists. I tried helping too, but my stepfather grabbed me and threw me towards the dinner table. I hit my head and hurt my shoulder. After that, I ran out of the house and hid in my favorite place, the tiny space above the chicken coop.

Feeling fear and helplessness as a child can be overwhelming. I learned at a very early age how families keep secrets, yet they really are not hidden. Secrets hide in the darkest part of your heart and come out in violent ways when provoked. I am not sure exactly what the secret was that my mother had shared with my stepfather, but it must have been bad.

We lived on a farm east of Booneville, Arkansas for three years before moving to Waveland, Arkansas, and at the foot of Mount Magazine. The house was a decent house. It was solid. It was not like a shack you would imagine a poor family in rural Arkansas would live in. We had a chicken coop, a large barn, and a few other wood shacks and smokehouse. I want to say, if my memory serves me correct, it was on about a hundred and sixty acres, in the country. Somebody from the Jehovah's Witness group had moved away and they rented it to us for a very little amount. For a few years, it felt like luxury accommodations.

When I was eight years old, I discovered a feral cat had taken refuge in one of our wood shacks. It was quickly after I found her, she had kittens. She had a bunch of kittens. I was so excited; I took one up to the house to show my mom. That was my first mistake. My stepfather became enraged. He marched all of us kids back outside, to the woodshed. One by one, he made us watch as he bashed the kitten's heads in with a large rock. I cried out for him to "please stop, I love them". He told me, "I already have to feed four of you kids, I can't afford to feed a bunch of kittens too". He went on to say, "sometimes, when you love something, you have to kill it, out of kindness".

This is where I learned a distorted view of love. It took years for me to realize, it was this man who was mentally ill and crazy, not others, or myself. I learned compassion at the deepest level of my core, from this experience. As I grew up, despite the fact, "kids were to be seen and not heard", I discovered my heart was a huge place to hold everything close that I loved. I swore to myself, when I became old enough, I would get away, and never come back. Every little bit of happiness I could find, whether it came from my friends, or my brother, stitched my soul back together.

I discovered over the years, it has been the smallest of happy events that have shaped me into who I am, today. It is not to say, all the trauma experienced as a child, isn't still there. What I want to say is, it does not have a hold on me. Pain can be the biggest catalyst for change you will ever find. Everyone experiences pain of some sort, during their life. It is how you rise above that, and fight for a different way of life, that sets you apart from the others.

My brother John and I both, found ways to feed ourselves from that point forward. I am not sure if it was out of fear of being bashed in the head with a rock, or we just needed to take care of ourselves. My brother made spears and we gigged for frogs. I was only eight years old, and he was ten. Both of my parents worked, and I was responsible for my two-year-old sister and my seven-year-old brother. We did not know much, and I found out very quickly, it is not easy trying to fry up a live frog. After the first attempt of cooking frog legs, my brother learned how to skin the frogs and cut just the legs off, so I could cook them. We were always hungry. We did what we needed to do, to eat. We fished a lot. We even cooked and ate fried fish eggs if the fish was a pregnant female. We even cooked mussels found at the bottom of our old pond. My brother hunted a lot of squirrels, rabbits, and later, deer. We learned to hunt only for what we needed to eat.

The very same thing happened when we learned kids in Africa ate large grasshoppers, and it was a delicacy. We filled a large coffee tin with the biggest grasshoppers we could find. We then dumped them into a large pot on the gas cook stove. I hurried and slammed a lid over the top. It only took a minute or two, to stop their thumping against the lid. When the grasshoppers were cooked, I slowly took the lid off. I told my brother I did not think I could eat them. But he was a genius. He found some Hershey's chocolate syrup. He soaked the fried grasshoppers with the chocolate syrup. They were very tasty. When I think back over this experience, I realize my brother never ate any of the grasshoppers. He did have a devilish smile on his face, however, and I realized I was a sucker. I was reminded of the time he gave me a huge bowl of night crawlers and told me, "don't eat them, BUT THEY SURE ARE GOOD!". I do not know why, but even today, I would jump off a bridge if my brother John asked me to. I love him that much. I suppose back then, it was brotherly love. He was ornery, but he always made me smile.

The summer I turned eleven we moved to Waveland, Arkansas. Looking back on this time of my life, it was the relationships I forged with friends from school and the neighbors in the countryside, that made the biggest impact on me. It was here I learned about hard work, kindness, respect, generosity, and how to have fun. I learned how important it is to dream of the life you want for yourself. I had dreams so big I never told anyone about, for fear they would tell someone, and it would never happen.

I found my voice when I was about twenty-one years old. I never really stopped talking after that. I wanted to be a writer. I dreamed of writing Harlequin romance novels. I wrote college research papers in the early nineteen eighties. Years ago, I wrote training programs for Diversity in the Workplace along with Time and Stress Management classes for several jobs I had. I did not write my own book until I turned sixty years old.

I had a fear of what people would say if I wrote the stories I needed to write. I do have to say, writing in a journal my entire life was very healing to me, but not near as healing as it was to publish my first book. Fear keeps us from doing so many things. It keeps us from applying for jobs we dream of. It keeps us from speaking out when we see or hear something we know is wrong. Fear of people seeing the real or true version of us keeps us quiet. So many people are walking around trying to be someone they are not. It is time we cut through the horse shit and be the real person we are. We can do this by sharing our stories. We can do this by being human. We can do this by being humble and admitting we do not know all the answers, but make a promise to find out, for the person asking. We can do this by doing the best job we can with the information we have. We can be open to learning new things. To be open to learning new things our whole lives is so crucial for surviving in this day and time. Everything changes so fast, all the time. It is important to keep up.

The very worst thing I ever did when I was a teenager was to cut all the watermelons off the vine of our neighbor's farm. I knew it was wrong, but I followed in my friend's footsteps anyway. Looking back, as an adult, I cannot even imagine the financial loss the farmer suffered that year. A year later, the farmer got cancer and he died. I know it was not my fault the farmer got cancer. But, for years, I felt he had a broken heart and just gave up because we destroyed his watermelon crop. I felt guilty for almost fifty years. Guilt can eat away at you like rust in a bucket. Soon, you have a hole in your heart where all the good things you truly deserve, fall through, because you do not believe you deserve any of them. Every person carries guilt of some sort. What is common among us all, is that it never leaves your mind. It is always there, chipping away at your soul, until you pull it out and deal with it. It is important to see it for what it is.

Kids of all ages, all genders, all races, do stupid things when they are growing up. There are lessons in all of them. The lesson I learned is to appreciate the hard work someone puts into a project, no matter what the project is. Whether it be a watermelon farm, or a marketing project, every person involved adds value to the project through their hard work. It must be appreciated. It must be valued. As a leader, if you do not do this, you are failing. You get a big fat F until you change your ways. Reach out and appreciate someone today. For a moment, pay attention to how their eyes light up and their posture changes. When you are genuine and sincere, people feel it. When a person feels valued, it goes straight to their heart. It is the cornerstone of building strong relationships.

In the same vein, a person's heart can break through one cruel deed or one cruel word. Being kind should be a priority in life for everyone. How can we make the people we work with feel better about their efforts, about themselves? How can we empower the people in our lives to be the best version of themselves? As leaders, it is our obligation, to build the best workforce the organization has ever had. We can do this by inspiring others. We can do this by being human. We can do this by being real, with everyone we meet.

I failed once. There are not enough pages to write the stories on about all my life's failures. I feel the only way to grow is to fail and keep failing. I am pretty darn good at it. I learn something so important every single time, I get excited about failing. Not really. Failing is painful. However, if you can fail and look for the lesson in the failure and use that to fail forward, you can become unstoppable. So far, we all have survived 100% of our failures. I like to say those are extremely good odds.

It is important to have a strong sense of self. It is important to not believe everything people say about you, believe the opinions people have of you, or even believe everything you hear. What other people say, is not necessarily true, so do not take it to heart. Whatever someone says about you, they are saying about themselves. It comes from their inner core about how they feel about themselves, most likely, struggles they are dealing with at the time. Also, when people cannot control you, they control how others see you. A lot of times, this is through misinformation. All it takes, is a little suggestion in someone's ear. It does not even have to be backed by facts. As a leader, it is your responsibility to nip this type of negative behavior in the bud. It is time, leaders have the courage to stand up for what is right and share their voice. If you happen to be one of these types of people, so you can turn the odds in your favor, shame on you.

It is a big mistake to believe negative things people say about you or to you. It is up to you, to get to know yourself. Constructive criticism is different. We are all open to improvement. It is the hateful people who are not happy with themselves that say things to hurt others, only to make themselves feel better. Most often, it is to keep the light from shining on them, for fear people will see what they have done, or what they are up to. There are a lot of people like this out there. It is important to have faith in your capabilities and talent. One area of my life, I have been afraid of pursuing, is my voice. For example, I love music. I grew up on Tammy Wynette, George Jones, Loretta Lynn, and classic rock and roll. One day, when I was ten years old, (1971) I was belting out, very loudly, a song by Three Dog Night. "Jeremiah was a bullfrog" was the name or what I thought the song's name was. It was a song partially written by Hoyt Axton. He never finished the song he called "Joy to the World". He was opening for Three Dog Night one year and they wrote the rest of the lyrics to the song. It became a number one hit back in the early nineteen seventies. It was originally written to inspire peace and love around the world, during a time of Vietnam. This was another reason this time period was so impressionable to us baby boomers.

I loved this song. I sang it all the time. One particular day, however, I was singing very loudly when I was told very sternly to "stop singing". "You can't sing" and "You have an awful voice". My stepfather told me "nobody wants to hear anything coming out of your mouth". The one thing I truly loved doing, was singing. I failed. I was a failure. I believed my stepfather's words about me. I was crushed. I never sang another song out loud, alone, until I was well into my fifties.

Words are powerful. Words can be crushing. What I learned from this is important. Before you speak, you need to choose your words carefully. What you say to someone can either make them or break them. When you are a leader, often you are speaking to large groups of people. Your impact will be felt by more than one person. Therefore, it is up to you to ensure you do not break people's spirit.

The other side of that coin is the louder you are, the more people will see you for who you truly are. A lot of people use their positions in society to make themselves feel important. They talk for the sake of talking. They talk over people. They make people feel inferior. They make people afraid to speak up. Most of the time, they talk just to hear themselves speak. What they are speaking is the same thing over and over in several different ways. A lot of times, these types of people are toxic and evil in nature, and usually a bully. If you pay attention, they bully their employees, their friends, their families, and even their peers. These types of people use fear to control others. These types of highbrows are an embarrassment wherever they go. These people are always conniving and trying to find ways to make other's look bad if it will help their cause of promoting themselves. It is a sad situation, because these types of people are the most insecure, lonely, people around. They are hurting inside, from whatever it was that made them this way. They cannot see it themselves, but they have a lot of unresolved issues and pain buried deep. In reality, these types of people need professional help. If you have someone like this in your organization, take a hard look and ask yourself if they cause more harm than good. If they have been around for years and that is why they are still there, ask yourself, what do they bring to the table and is it worth it? No matter what you do in your organization to create healthy employees, healthy environments, and healthy cultures, keeping this type of person around will undermine everything you are striving for. They can poison your organization. They can ruin your reputation.

There are so many ways to deliver bad news, whether it is a whole group, or just one employee. You need to find a way to encourage and inspire people at all costs. You cannot do this cleanly if you have a pile of unresolved issues of your own. As a leader, it is imperative you deal with your own issues in a healthy way and get them out of the way, so you can grow and be a teacher of excellence to those who follow you. Leaders must have the highest emotional intelligence they can, to move into the future role of holistic leadership. As leaders, it is imperative we keep our instincts sharp, our minds clear, so we can tune in to the people around us. It helps us, help others.

Being centered, calm, at peace, is critical for making better decisions, taking the right roads, and becoming a great leader. Leaders must do whatever it takes to keep their instincts intact. This helps when dealing with crisis issues or employees who are in crisis mode. Leaders who develop routines for themselves to cope with their own stress, are light years ahead of others who do not place their own emotional wellbeing first. When creating holistic wellness programs for your organization, it is exciting when a leader works with employees from the ground up. This is a perfect time to share your own story or to find a way to connect with your people on a human level. You would be surprised how many people fear leadership. Take that fear away. Be real. Be human. Be kind. It is time that leadership serves the people, not the other way around.

Chapter 1 – Introduction

In 2019, only three years ago, the cost of unhealthy people at work was a 2.2 trillion-dollar loss in the United States alone. This was 12% of the GDP. The breakdown of that is as follows: $1,100 billion dollars costs of chronic disease; $250 billion dollars cost of work-related injuries; $300 billion dollars costs of work-related stress; $550 billion dollars cost of disengagement of work. These statistics should grab your attention. Without employees, there would not be an organization. Leaders forget about this. Not only do they forget about it, but they also do not give much thought on how employees drive the success or failure of an organization.

Until recently, most organizations are focused on a profit-based business model. The bottom line is, how much money can we make? In many instances, it does not matter how the bottom line was received, or how the employees are treated to hit that profit margin goal. Times are changing all around the world. It is time to pay attention. Paying attention to the people that make a company is not only smart, but a necessity.

In the past, employee assistance programs were created to help employees adjust through periods of organizational transition. In the past, employees suffered through RIF, layoffs, furloughs, and pay cuts. It is very difficult to regain the respect of employees once you have lost it, no matter what you do. We are in a time of a lot of closures. Organizations that have been around for decades are closing. People are being laid off or terminated. Many other organizations are cutting positions. Some organizations are cutting hours. Organizations that do have employee assistance programs are a step ahead. It is a base to begin working from when upgrading existing programs to a more holistic program.

There is evidence that proves when employees are valued, engaged, respected, and trusted, they work harder, smarter, are more loyal, which in turn increases productivity, profitability, and lowers turnover within organizations (Alhamami, Ismail, Kamarudin & Abdullah, 2020). The technology revolution along with globalization has changed the very face of business dramatically. The world is the stage and countries are coming together to define sustainability and social responsibility.

In today's business world, it is crucial to create a culture of leadership that is strong and based upon transparency, honesty, respect, and a model of unshakable ethics (Solinger,

Jansen & Cornelissen, 2020). Leaders must walk their talk. Relationships take time to build. It is important employees learn and know they matter within an organization (Pasha & Rehman, 2020). Employees take care of customers. Leaders take care of employees. Leadership should develop clear and strategic goals for the organization that is clearly understood and supported by all. The goals of an organization should include building the best workforce they have ever had in the history of the company. Investing in the employees to develop future leaders within the organization is crucial. Creating an environment of openness will inspire employees to become engaged and creative towards problem solving and finding real workable solutions for the company.

Leaders of today should be creating teams of excellence. Employees who feel they are valued for their knowledge and expertise will be more open to sharing that knowledge and expertise with new employees who do not know as much. It is important to get to know employees, their strengths, their weaknesses, their goals, and ambitions. Incorporating continuing educational opportunities for all employees will demonstrate the organizational investment and value of all. Employees want to know what they do every day is making a difference (Pasha & Rehman, 2020). Leaders who lead by gratitude and being of service to others transform organizations (Bachelder, 2018).

While leaders of the past have focused solely upon profits to gauge success in business, profits alone do not measure the true success of an organization. True success is a result of emotional intelligence among leaders and employees as demonstrated by how a leader inspires, motivates, serves, intellectually stimulates, trusts, and respects his/her employees. The strength of the organization is as strong as the strength of the relationships developed within and the legacy left behind once the leader has gone. A good place to start is the wellness of the whole person. The whole person includes leadership. There are many dimensions of wellness in a person, but there are seven main distinct areas that should be balanced to become totally well. These areas include career/occupational, spirituality, financial, family/environmental, social, creativity/intellectual, and health/physical.

The next several chapters will break down these seven dimensions of wellness. I will also add a few others into the mix I feel are important. The one thing to remember, if nothing else, is change starts with leadership. As a leader, I want you to apply each of these following chapters to yourself. Take a good look at where you are in life. Make the needed changes, then move forward. It can be painful to do this. It is so much easier to put one foot in front of the other and keep marching on as usual. Life is hard. Change is hard. But you are worth every second of it. I want you to remember that. It is easier to live a life you love than to be miserable. You will add years to your life if you allow joy to fill you in every aspect.

As you are reading this book, think about how to drive excellence in your own organization. Every single employee is so much more than what you see. And so are you. You are more than what people see. When people begin to embrace wholeness and wellness in the workplace, the benefits begin showing up in the way morale is improving, saving money, and reducing sick leave. A lot of times, it is as simple as moving forward with a healthy way of living, good nutrition, physical activity, and mental wellness. It is important to get to know who is working for you and give them a taste of who you are. It works both ways. Be vulnerable, open, respectful, humble, and eager to learn yourself. It is true, we do not know everything. It takes a diverse group of people with a multitude of different talents and skills to bring excellence together.

Chapter 2-The Whole Person-Career-Occupational

Today, leaders are transforming the world of leadership through building strong relationships, strong teams, transparency, trust, and strategic planning, to create the best workforce ever. It is extremely important to look beyond what an employee can do, but more at who the employee is, as a whole person. But first, let us look at leadership. Let's look at the dimension of career.

As a leader, I want you to ask yourself, are you happy? If not, why not? Be honest with yourself. No one is here but you. If you are not thrilled at the end of the day, or inspired by everything you and your team accomplished, maybe you are not following your passion. Your work should be in direct alignment with your heart and the goals you have established for yourself. This area of career is important because you will spend one third of your life doing the work you choose. That is right. You get to choose your work, or your career. If you have invested tens of thousands of dollars in an education, so you can pursue this career and yet, you are not happy, why are you staying?

Maybe this career is not what you thought it would be. Maybe things have changed over the years, and it is not that rewarding or fun any longer. It is okay to change directions. It is never too late to follow your heart's path. It does not matter what it is. Who cares if you change directions? It should only matter to you because you are just as important as everyone else. You are only on this earth for a very short time period. Make sure, you choose the path that brings you the most joy. All is not lost. Think of the lessons and the relationships you have built to bring you to this point in your life. But, before you quit your job, look around in your company and see if there is a better path, a better fit for you. If not, then decide to make a change. A leader who oozes happiness or joy with themselves can only inspire those following.

I say this for one reason only. Your people know when you are not happy. Your people can see it written all over your face and in everything you do. This energy you share filters down to everyone. Your words, your actions, all tell a story. The story you want to tell should be the fire in your belly that gets you so damn excited to be where you are, making a difference. If you have lost your passion, do something about it. Maybe, it is just a matter of taking some time off and spending time with yourself or someone you love. Maybe, you are not challenged any longer. Maybe, nothing excites you anymore. Find something that does. Believe me, it is never too late to follow your heart. If you have forgotten what that is, think of a time, when you were younger and stress free. What did you get excited about? What did you dream about? What inspired you? Life is not about the money you make or the things you have acquired. It is about the relationships you have nurtured and built along the way. It is about how you feel about yourself. If you feel you have lost your spark, do something to light that fire back up.

When I graduated from the Integrative Nutrition School, one of the things I learned was, that finding joy in your career is what they call "primary food" (Institute of Integrative Nutrition, 2016). It is what feeds your soul. That is the loaded question. What feeds your soul? When a person feeds the different aspects of their lives with things that inspires them and bring them joy, they become more whole. When a person is more whole and balanced, then the stress, anxiety, depression, weight gain, weight loss, and other issues are tiny compared to being overwhelming or unmanageable. When a person is whole and well, they think smarter, make better choices, see things clearer, have higher emotional intelligence, and their passion flows through them and out towards every person they meet, sharing joy and inspiration.

That is also a great question to ask your employees when you are getting to know them. Asking what a person is passionate about will tell you a lot. It is possible, if you feel you have lost your passion or inspiration, and you still love what you do, that you are just tired. Being tired or having feelings of burnout is very common among leaders. If that is the case, take a vacation. Go somewhere you have never been. It is time to unplug for a while. I mean, really unplug. Work will be there when you get back. Do not ever forget, you are important, also. Your employees will thank you. Your family will thank you. Your body will thank you.

Chapter 3-The Whole Person-Spirituality

Everyone believes in something or someone. Spirituality is a very personal thing. Some people feel stronger about their faith than others do. To many people, spirituality is connected to their religion. To other people, spirituality is connected to living a meaningful life. To some people, it is about connecting to something bigger than themselves. To others, it might be just finding a calm center within to meditate and find an inner peace. When it comes to leadership, it is important to embrace spirituality in the workplace. This allows employees to feel what they do has meaning and is worthwhile. It brings value to the employee. It also demonstrates the organizational support of spirituality in the workplace.

When looking at the whole person and the dimension of spirituality, it is easy to judge. Let's not judge each other. Let's embrace the diversity all around us. It is not for us to judge whether someone is leading a spiritual life or not. It is not for us to judge whether a person's faith is bigger or better than ours. It is not for us to judge how a person prays or how a person reaches out for spiritual strength or help. The best thing we can do is offer a quiet place, support, in a time of need.

People are hurting. People are experiencing pain in a million different ways. Most people do not want to talk about what is on their hearts for fear of retribution or judgment. The important thing for a leader to know is they have the power to make changes in the workplace. Creating a quiet place that can offer a moment's peace or joy to others, can be a lifeline. You may not know someone has thoughts of suicide. You may not know someone has lost a child, a parent, or a spouse. You may not know someone is struggling just to get through one more day, alone. You may not know someone is struggling with addiction, or cancer. You may not know someone was abused or is living in a house full of domestic violence. Not every person is strong. Sometimes, it is the one's you think are the strongest, that need that one moment, more than anyone else.

Spirituality is not always about religion. It is about connection. Many people do different things to feel connected to something bigger than themselves, or to still their mind and find calmness. I have found that people who believe in a higher power, can find comfort when they are in need.

Sometimes, that is the only thing they have left. People have their own ways of coping. People have their own ways of clinging to hope when there is nothing left. There are many ways to feel connected to something that feeds your faith.

Let's take Yoga, for example. Yoga is a very old and complex practice. It is rooted in Indian philosophy. It began as a spiritual practice years ago but has been widely accepted in the western world and is very popular as a way to promote mental and physical wellbeing. Typically, yoga that is practiced in the United States includes physical postures called (asanas) along with breathing techniques called (pranayanna) and includes meditation (dyana). There are many different styles of yoga ranging from easy to strenuous and advanced. There is also yoga practiced with two types of Eastern (Chinese origin) meditative movements called Tai Chi and Qi Gong.

All of the yoga and meditative movements promote mental and physical wellbeing. Yoga relieves stress, promotes good sleep and balance, improves mental and emotional health. It also helps people manage difficult life situations, stress, anxiety, and depression. Many people support the yoga routine or lifestyle because it helps with chronic illness, back and neck pain, headaches, and overall mental or spiritual health.

If you are thinking of Yoga as an answer to a health issue, it is recommended you consult with your physician first. Some people might find the yoga postures very difficult to do. Every person is different. If you have a lot of serious health issues, it is good to ask your physician's opinion on trying something new. Many organizations are offering free yoga classes to their employees. Some organizations are offering quiet peaceful areas where individuals can do yoga on their lunch breaks or even before or after hours, alone. Many organizations offer a small sanctuary for privacy or a moment's peace. Many people find joy or comfort in yoga. Yoga can also fall into the dimension of spirituality or dimension of health.

So far, we have covered only two dimensions of the whole person, career, and spirituality. Ask yourself how you would rank, from 1 to 10, 10 being the best, your joy with your career compared to your joy with your spirituality. If you rank a 5 with your career and a 10 with your spirituality, then you can see there is an imbalance between the two wellness dimensions. Your career needs a little attention. Or it could be the opposite. Maybe you need to spend more time finding something that brings you joy in the wellness dimension of spirituality. This could be anything from reading a book on spirituality, adding a daily prayer to your routine, finding a likeminded group of people to connect with, or even embracing meditation into your daily routine. You are in charge of your life. You get to make the decisions of what brings you joy.

Balance is the key. Many organizations are embracing life-work balance. Some organizations are offering four-day work weeks to help employees find balance in the rest of their lives. This is a great start. Some organizations allow employees to work from home for a day or two each week. Of course, this depends on your role within the organization. If you are a receptionist, that would be impossible. There are many other things organizations can offer, also. Employees have great ideas. It is always a great time when employees come together with leadership and brainstorm about wellness in the workplace ideas.

Career development plans and career development departments help employees to keep learning and bettering themselves, often creating the next generation of leadership for the organization. This ties into creating meaningful work for the employee, which can fall into the spirituality dimension of wellness. When an employee feels the organization believes in him/her enough to invest time and money for a career development plan, they feel valued. In turn, they will become more productive, more loyal, more passionate about the organization and how they fit in.

A transformational leader will take the time to get to know his/her employees. It is during this time; employees can share their passions and goals. Leaders can see the strengths and weaknesses of the employee and work on balancing out the areas. It is possible, a person is just working for a paycheck. There is nothing wrong with this, especially, if they do their job and do it well. This ties into the generational differences in values that I spoke about in Part I. It depends what generation the employee comes from, as to whether career development is important to them or not. It also is possible; the employee is working to fulfill a spiritual need of meaningful work.

Chapter 4 -The Whole Person- Financial

I am a firm believer the topic of finances and money management should be taught in grade school. It would be amazing if real life skills were taught to everyone. It would help a lot of people as they grow into adulthood, to make better decisions.

Many people live above their means. People have this grand idea of what they want people to believe about them. To some people, life is all about appearances. So, they buy the big houses, vacation homes, fancy cars, clothes, jewelry, and vacations. Most, of which, they cannot afford. They are constantly talking about their titles, their promotions, how much they spend, the money they earn. Nobody likes a braggart. That will be the mark you leave behind. It is wonderful if you can afford this, and you choose to do so. You have earned it. You can live a classy lifestyle. There is nothing wrong with driving a classy car. I am talking to the people who live month to month and tie up credit cards with high interest rates, just to live the lifestyle above their means. It is an addiction. It is a very stressful addiction. The deeper you wrap yourself in this facade, the more transparent you become to everyone around you. The more stress you create for yourself. You might even call it shallow, fake, and selfish.

A lot of people earn a very good wage, yet it takes every penny to pay the minimum balances on the credit card, even as the limits are increasing. It is very unhealthy to constantly compete with everyone and everything around you. The only person you need to compete against, is yourself. Make it a lifelong goal to be better than you were yesterday. When you finally realize this, the stress will fall away. In the long scheme of things, people do not care. What people will remember about you, is how you made them feel every time you were in their company. After a while, you will wake up and realize you may not have many true friends. It is up to you to leave a legacy of kindness, respect, and gratitude.

It is possible, you are just trying to give your family everything you never had. Maybe, you have four kids in college. Everything costs more than it did in the past. It is easy to borrow money from Peter to pay Paul. We all do it at some point in our lives. However, It can create an enormous amount of stress for you. Once again, stress causes heart disease, cancer, anxiety, and depression. If you can look at your finances in a realistic way and make the changes that are needed, you will be better off in the long run.

I did not really learn about money management until I obtained my MBA. What I have learned is how NOT knowing about money management can ruin you. There are many free programs in every state that offer educational classes on money management. Even the SBA (Small Business Administration) have online webinars that are very educating. They are worth checking out.

The big question is: Does your financial situation bring you joy? If not, maybe it is time to sit down and make a list of assets and liabilities you might have. Maybe, it is time to get rid of all your credit cards except one or two. It is good to have one in case of an emergency, or even great to have when you travel. Develop a plan to pay off the credit card debt. Do you own vacation homes in other states, but it has been years since you had time off to visit? If so, and you want to keep them, you can check into ways of turning that asset into a money-making asset and not a liability.

I have a friend who is elderly. Fifty years ago, he and his wife bought land and a cabin in Colorado. In the beginning, they would go a couple of times a year and stay for a week. After five years, they went only once during the summer. When they went for vacation, they spent their entire vacation cleaning up the property grounds. Mowing, weed eating, and cutting firewood for the next trip, next year, was a lot of work. The cost of property taxes and insurance was high. In the end, they sold the property for less than what they had invested in it over the fifty-year period.

It is nice to own something, like a mountain home in Colorado. However, it is wiser to think of the financial long-term aspect of the decision and weigh the pros and cons before investing. A person could take many trips to Colorado and stay in the finest of places for less than what their cost was every year. If you do have a vacation home that is not being utilized for most of the year, and you want to keep it, turn it into a money-making vacation rental.

Most married couples that divorce, divorce because of financial problems. Arguments over money is very common. When a person is carrying a burden of financial stress, it bleeds over into every relationship he/she has. It is very difficult to turn a financial situation around. This is mainly because a person usually has one job with one income. If married, then most of the time, there are two incomes, but still not enough to cover everything. The cost of living has increased substantially. The cost of college, food, clothes, housing, fuel, doctor bills, insurance, utilities, and vehicles are only a few of the staples people need. Even as we speak, people are suffering, financially. Many people have too much pride to ask for help.

There are some people who work hard and turn over their entire paychecks to the spouse to handle. Then, when they need money, they have to ask for it, like a child. If you are one of these people, then be honest about how this makes you feel. Everyone needs money of their own and money as a couple. This might be as simple as depositing a certain amount in a joint account to handle all the necessities and each spouse have an individual account. I have known people who are in situations like this and see their resentment towards their spouse. It is an unnecessary resentment that can be handled in such an easy way. If the resentment festers over years, it can eventually end up as a reason for a divorce, despite loving someone. It is so important to be transparent with your spouse, especially about finances. It paves the way for a smoother road along the way, and a stronger bond with your partner.

My husband and I both worked over eighty hours a week each, for about ten years. During this time, we ate out two or three times a day because we were never home. It was convenient. We spent an enormous amount of money at restaurants, not to mention the type of unhealthy food we put into our bodies during this time. When you have the income coming in, it is not that big of a deal, still not smart, but not as much an issue. But I think about the tens of thousands of dollars spent over ten years we could have put into a savings or investment account. Hindsight is twenty-twenty. Those ten years are gone. It is extremely important to be smart about money management.

It is also important to regularly check your credit reports. Identity theft is at an all-time high. Most banks also, offer a program that is usually under ten dollars a month. The program monitors your credit report for possible fraud or identity theft attempts. It is worth the investment. I have discovered my identity has been stolen several times over the past twenty years. It was very painful to discover my identity had been stolen by my own family members. Never give your social security number to anyone, unless it is the bank. People can tell you any reason they want to, just to get your social security number. Due diligence is critical. It is better to know, than not to know.

This is a hot topic that can be added to your organizational wellness program. It can be through digital education, or even classroom continuing education. You would be shocked at the number of people who do not have a clue about managing money. Financial issues are huge stressors for anybody. As a leader, you have an opportunity to help people in this area. Many organizations offer retirement choices. The average person does not know a lot about investing. There are also many organizations that will come speak to employees about investment opportunities and about the different types available.

As a leader, it is a great time to assess your own financial stability. The big question again is, does your financial wellness bring you joy? It is extremely important that you are satisfied and feeling secure about your financial wellness. If you are not sure where you stand, you can create a vision board of what you want your financial wellness to look like. It is crucial you become very mindful and strategic in your investments and planning. It is important to increase your revenue and decrease your cost in all areas. Be very clear with yourself about short-term goals and long-term goals. Get rid of what you do not want. Keep what you do want. It is simple as that. It is a perfect time to clean out the clutter. You can make donations to so many nonprofit organizations in your community. It is time to clean out the old and make way for the new to enter your life.

How does your dimension of financial wellness rank next to your career and spirituality dimensions? It is important all three should be balanced equally. If not, make the adjustments needed to get them into alignment that brings you joy. If you are married, have an honest, sit-down discussion about where you really are financially. It is better to make decisions together, if you value each other and want to stay together. A lot of times, the primary breadwinner will keep things hidden, especially financial stress, to protect the spouse. The spouse will feel valued and appreciated if they know the true financial situation and become a partner in finding the appropriate solutions to financial issues that need to be addressed.

Most people already know where they stand financially. Imbalance in the financial dimension can affect wellness markers in health such as stress, weight, and energy levels. I have had many times in my life, where I was stressed about the lack of money. For me, it shows up in weight gain. What I realized, years later, is how I used food to comfort me. I used it as a security blanket. What I fed my body, was the only thing I could control. The most I have weighed in my life was 325 lbs. I reached this unbelievable weight at the hardest time in my life. As an adult, the least I have weighed was 115. My healthiest weight was around 140. It is important to find a healthy way to cope with stress. The first forty-five years of my life, I was a runner. Exercise, whether it is walking, running, or cycling, or some other form, is extremely important for your overall health. When I began pulling out the pile of my life's personal challenges and working through each of them, my weight began to drop. I began to feel better. I am still a work in progress. We all are. Take back your life. Clean out your emotional traumas, pain, experiences, and make room to be the person you were born to be.

It is a perfect opportunity, however, for you to assess your financial dimension. Look at your physical body. Have you gained a lot of weight? Have you lost a lot of weight? Do you have issues with eating healthy foods or filling your meals with unhealthy foods? Taking an honest look at your weight, will shed a light on you. Everything you put into your body, is either feeding chronic disease or building a strong house for your soul to live and thrive in.

The ultimate goal is to identify obstacles or challenges and make decisions to be happy. Are you truly happy with your financial wellness? Do what needs to be done to bring this dimension of wellness back into alignment with your own personal goals in life. You deserve to live a fulfilled and joyful life, free of stress.

Chapter 5 -The Whole Person-Family-Environmental

As a leader, when looking at the whole person, it is more than each dimension of wellness. It is a focus on anything that can affect a person's health. This would include a healthy or unhealthy weight, anxiety, depression, lack of energy, or high stress. A person that is healthy, cares about what kind of nutrition they feed their bodies, how much physical activity they get every week, the health of all their relationships, and the overall lifestyle they choose to live.

I come from a different type of family life than most people. Therefore, I have a different view of family and the kinds of stress it can bring. I would love to believe there are many more healthy families out there in the world, than unhealthy ones. What I do know, surprisingly, is that all families have issues of some kind or another. It is not really important to focus on why or who, but more importantly, how the issue makes you feel. If being around family brings you stress, anxiety, depression, or pain, then it will be one of the dimensions in your wellness that needs to be addressed. You do not owe anyone anything. However, you owe yourself everything. Focus on your own personal wellness. Wellness on the inside will reflect on wellness on the outside.

As a leader, I want you to be honest about assessing your family wellness dimension. A lot of times, sibling rivalry carries through adulthood. At some point, you must decide how important it is. There are a lot of things that will never change or cannot be changed. When you do not have any control over things like that, then it is in your best interest, to let it go. Also, if you come from a blended family, it can bring tensions. Sometimes, it is a matter of talking to the person and sharing how you feel. Many people are totally unaware, and it might be lack of communication or miscommunication that causes stress or anxiety. If it is something simple as that, make time to get it straightened out. You need to get back on track. You will feel so much better about yourself.

If you experienced feelings of abandonment or loss of a parent at an early age, you must pull this out and deal with it. It can be excruciatingly painful. You must realize you are not responsible for anyone else. You are not responsible for other people's choices, decisions, or actions. What other people choose to do with their lives, is their burden to carry, not yours. You are not the reason for abandonment. This can be a heavy burden to carry throughout your life. Many times, decisions that family members make, are made during stressful times in their lives. Many times, it is survival instincts and they do not think of the long term affects it will have on their children or other family members. Letting go of this type of life experience can be exhilarating. It will relieve a tremendous amount of stress from your life when you realize you are only responsible for you. You can hold onto old hurtful memories, or you can use it as fuel to fight for a better life for yourself and your family. You can use it to repair damage in existing family relationships.

Does your dimension of family wellness bring you joy? If so, you are very blessed. A long time ago, it was easier for me to focus on my immediate family, like my own sons. When I think of my two sons and my daughter-n-laws, and my four grandchildren, I want to burst with joy and pride. I am so proud of my family. I am so very proud of the family each of my sons have created themselves.

I come from a very broken family system. I learned a long time ago; I am not responsible for the choices my family members have made or the roads they choose to go down. I can only be responsible for myself and the family that I create.

It is the only way I have been able to make peace and find comfort. I have relationships with the family members I want to have relationships with. Over the years, I have reached out and stayed very close to the family that is important to me. I do not put effort into family relationships that are only one sided.

As a certified International Health Coach, I want to reiterate how important primary foods are. Again, primary foods are not really food, but it is what feeds your soul (Institute of Integrative Nutrition, 2016). It is what makes you happy. It is what brings you joy, comfort, and peace. The dimension of wellness in the family group is a primary food. So, here we are again, the big question is, does your family dimension bring you joy? How does it rank compared to your financial, spiritual, and career dimension? If it is out of balance, then add it to your list of things to address. If it is at the top 10 and brings you joy, then you are in a very blessed spot.

As a leader, it is important to know your employees. Most of the time, employees will keep their family life private. It is easy to gauge, if an employee is showing signs of stress, anxiety, depression, weight loss or weight gain, there might be a problem at home or with family. Taking the time to let that person know, they matter to the organization, and you are there to help in any way you can, says a lot. Most people will keep silent and struggle alone because they fear people will think less of them. It is during times such as these, support shown to an employee or coworker can make all the difference in the world.

There are so many topics that fall in the family category, that can be added to the holistic employee wellness programs. Topics that can be included could touch on sensitive areas such as domestic violence, addiction, mental health, financial assistance, coping with loss, divorce, housing assistance, childcare assistance, food, healthcare, aging parents, and even transportation assistance. Organizations can reach out to local community organizations for healthy resources to share. The important thing is to let the employee know they matter. It is important the employee know there is someone who cares, and they are not alone. It is a great opportunity to include employees when making decisions on the topics needed to complete your new wellness initiative. It might even be an eye opener to learn what employees truly value and what topics are truly needed.

I also want to say the topic of addiction is more than alcohol or drugs. It can include things like sugar addiction, sexual addiction, lying, stealing, smoking, and possibly even hoarding. All these things are unhealthy and will affect your dimension in family/environmental wellness.

Chapter 6 -The Whole Person-Social

I love people. I would say I am a very social person. I have a very healthy dimension of social well-being. I also love my privacy. I enjoy my own company. I enjoy being around family and friends. I enjoy dining alone. I enjoy dining with friends and family. A lot of people, mostly family, think I am depressed when I hibernate at home. The truth of the matter is, I love having the time to create new goals and a better me.

Some people are shy. Some people are outgoing. It is a good time to check your social dimension of wellness and rate yourself. Maybe, if you rank it low, then it is a good time to address the needs you have and bring the score back into balance with your whole self. Do you have a social circle of friends? Do you make time to get out of the house and mingle with other people, every now and then? Do you have friends? Are you afraid of putting yourself out there, for fear of rejection? Does your life consist of going to work and going home, day in and day out? What do you do for yourself, that makes you happy?

There have been many times in my life, however, when I not only wanted to be alone, but needed to be alone. A person can only take so much, of whatever it is. Life is hard. Life can be challenging. When I left Oklahoma and traveled to Alaska twenty-two years ago, I needed to be alone. What actually happened, though, I ended up meeting people along the way that filled my soul with joy. I met people who inspired me to find my true path in life. I found that I could be that person who lived a remote life, away from people. I found I could go to town once or twice a year for supplies and be happy with myself. But, the truth of the matter is, everyone needs to feel they are not alone in the world. It is crucial to unplug occasionally, to keep your instincts sharp. It is not healthy to isolate yourself completely, from the rest of the world, for long periods of time. It is important to build strong relationships as we go through life. It is through these relationships and bonds that will sustain us during hard times.

During my second marriage, my husband did not want me to be around my family, friends, or people I worked with. It was a very debilitating relationship. It was a very controlling relationship. There are many people today that are in these types of relationships. When this happens, the social dimension is out of whack. The person gets dependent solely on the spouse. They lose their self-confidence. They lose family and friends that were important to them. It is critical to be balanced in the social dimension. It is important for couples to have relationships as couples and friendships and social contact as individuals, outside of the relationship. It takes a lot of faith, trust, and respect towards each other to embrace this and want the spouse to have wholesome and healthy social relationships. Our goal should be to help our partner be the best version of themselves they can be.

As a leader, it is easy to spot an employee that might be suffering in the social wellness dimension. They are often unable to make basic decisions without first asking their spouse or partner. They are often employees who keep to themselves for fear of upsetting someone at home or even at work. They also usually lack self-esteem and self-confidence. These are areas that a leader can help build upon by letting the employee know they matter.

Leaders can embrace this type of employee and give them a little extra responsibility to build their confidence and self-esteem. Praise and recognition go a lot farther than you may realize. It does not have to be at an annual employee recognition ceremony, it can be praise given quietly anytime it is deserved. You will see an employee blossom right before your eyes when their self-confidence begins to grow. They will remember your kindness, and your efforts.

There is the other end of the spectrum, also. People who can only thrive in a social environment. A lot of times, these people are afraid to be alone. They are not happy in their own skin. They are not happy alone. It is a perfect time to evaluate where you stand on the social dimension of wellness. If you are not happy being alone, find out why. Try to get back into balance with who you truly are.

This might be as simple as finding a hobby or resurrecting an old dream you had as a child. Maybe, you wanted to be a writer when you were a kid. Maybe, you wanted to paint, do woodwork, or even garden. Pursuing hobbies or old dreams will help you as an adult, to balance out the social wellness dimension. Treat yourself, once a week, to a dinner alone, but at a popular restaurant. This will, in time, help balance out this area of social wellbeing, if you are a loner. Visit an art store, or garden center, or lumber yard. You will soon meet people who will help you pursue other aspects of your life, all the while, bringing your social wellbeing into alignment.

Chapter 7 -The Whole Person- Creativity-Intellectual

Many people are naturally creative and artists. Many people dream of being creative and artistic but let fear of rejection keep them from opening this well inside of them. A lot of people, like me, buy paint and paint brushes and easels and canvas and let it sit for ten to twelve years before making the time to pursue it. The truth of the matter is, we are all artists. Every single person has the potential inside of them to create something beautiful.

It is important to make time in your life to be creative. It doesn't have to be with canvas and paint. It can be with wood, metal, paper, gardens, ceramics, or anything that brings out the creative artist in you. Some people pursue writing. That is also a creative outlet. Maybe you have always wanted to learn how to play the guitar, piano or sing. There is no time like the present.

Think of yourself and honestly rank where you are with your intellectual and creative dimension. If you are lacking, make a list of things you would like to do. Maybe it is taking the time to refinish an old piece of furniture, or birdhouse, or beehive. Maybe, you want to buy flagstone and dig out an area in your back yard for a private oasis. Maybe you want to build a canoe or cabin. Maybe you want to fly a plane. Whatever you dream of doing, make the time to at least start it. You will surprise yourself. There are many places that give lessons or instructions on how to do things if you research in your community. A lot of hobby stores will have classes on bow making, watercolor painting, wood working, and many other things.

The important thing is to get moving in the creative dimension. It will bring joy, lessen any stress you might be having, and remind you how talented you really are. If you are shy, ask a friend to go with you or help you. It is a great way to spend time with family or friends. It will also bring new people into your life. Do what brings you joy.

Many times, people wish they had gone back to college but never pursue it for fear they are too old. Age is a mindset. If you are breathing, you can still pursue any dream you have. I was fifty-seven when I went back to college and fifty-nine when I graduated with an MBA. The feelings this gave to me are indescribable. When I was growing up, we did not have money for food, let alone, continuing education or college.

When I was raising my sons alone, it was the same situation. I worked all the time to pay the bills. There was never any extra money left over. My sons took advantage of the high school programs and community vocational centers to gain advanced knowledge in specialized areas. This prepared them for great jobs. They both made more money that I ever did. I always wished I could have paid for college for my sons when they were young. Not everyone wants to go to college. There are so many jobs out there that do not require a degree. Many of these jobs pay extremely well. What I want to say to anyone reading this, is it is never too late to go back to school, especially, if you want to change directions in your career, or even to become more knowledgeable about a particular topic.

As a leader, evaluate your creativity/intellectual dimension. If it is balanced with the other dimensions, then you are in a sweet spot. If not, make the necessary decisions and go after whatever brings you joy.

Chapter 8 -The Whole Person-Health-Physical

Every person should know exactly how healthy they are. If you have not had a physical in years, it is time. It is important to have a complete blood work drawn to include CBC, CMP, thyroid, and liver tests. This should be done yearly. Once you receive your results from your physician, you can make a plan on what you need to do next.

It is important to have preventive tests done to stay ahead of any diseases, especially if you are over forty, such as colonoscopy, mammograms, annual physicals, dental work, and vision checks. Many hospitals offer wellness checks that include checking for aneurysms, blood clots, heart problems, and blood pressure.

Whether you are in leadership or an employee, everyone has stress. Stress causes cancer, heart attacks, strokes, high blood pressure, shingles, and many other chronic diseases. You must make time for you. You deserve to be healthy. A lot of people think they are healthy, only to discover they are not. It is good to get a professional exam to have a baseline to build from.

The health and physical dimension of wellness is critical for overall function. I was a long-distance runner for almost forty years. I never worried about what I ate because my level of physical activity kept me thin. It wasn't until I had a job where I sat for long periods at a computer, and I did not make physical activity a priority, did I begin to have stress in my life. This turned into weight gain, which brought a whole addition of health issues to my door.

It is important to get moving. Even if it is for ten minutes a day. When you get to feeling good about those ten minutes, then add another ten minutes to your activity. Before you know it, you will be routinely walking a mile or two or more every day. If you are overweight, or just want to drop ten pounds or so, walking will help.

Honestly rate where you stand in your health dimension. If it is low, then make the necessary adjustments to get moving. A lot of organizations offer exercise rooms or facilities for employees. If your organization is small, check with local work out facilities and look for company discounts to give your employees. Many employees will take half of their lunch hour and walk together. It helps the time go by and keeps their hearts in good shape. Other organizations will turn vacant space into exercise rooms with treadmills and other equipment for employees to use for free. This is another way to demonstrate to employees how they are valued. It is even better when leadership makes time to stay healthy also.

If you are like me, and it has been a while since you exercised, take it slow. Keep a log and jot down the minutes you walked and the distance. Before you know it, you will be competing against yourself, trying to beat your own record. Do whatever it takes to make yourself feel good about you again.

Get involved in the local community and get physical. Perhaps there are adult soccer, baseball, basketball, or even pickle ball sports that are looking for additional players. The YMCA is also a great place to get moving and to meet people. They offer aerobics and exercise classes before work and after work hours. If you have children, they usually have a daycare on site, also.

The bottom line is everyone knows what needs to be done. It is having the discipline and courage to do it. Exercise lowers your cholesterol, strengthens the heart, lowers sugar levels, builds muscle, and burns fat, among many other things. The endorphins that are released in your brain when you exercise are the "I feel good" feelings that lift your mood and will help relieve stress of any kind. The better you begin to feel, the more you begin to incorporate physical activity back into your lifestyle. The more it brings you closer to the true you.

If you get back on track and then get off track for a period, do not beat yourself up over it. Just start back up. It is your body, your health, your life. Do something that brings you joy. It might be just taking the dogs for a walk after work. Whatever you decide, you will be glad you made the decision to get moving again.

If you think you don't have time to get healthy, think of the time you will have to spend when you are ill, not to mention, the time off of work and costs of medicine and doctor bills.

In 2019, only three years ago, the cost of unhealthy people at work was a 2.2 trillion-dollar loss in the United States alone. This was 12% of the GDP. The breakdown of that is as follows: $1,100 billion dollars costs of chronic disease; $250 billion dollars cost of work-related injuries; $300 billion dollars costs of work-related stress; $550 billion dollars cost of disengagement of work. These statistics should grab your attention. Without employees, there would not be an organization. Leaders forget about this. Not only do they forget about it, they do not give much thought on how employees drive the success or failure of an organization.

It makes sense for us to do whatever we can to keep our employees healthy and happy. This is not only for employees; it is for leaders also.

When comparing your health dimension to the rest of your whole wellness, how does it rank? Have you made the time for yourself to be healthy? Do you incorporate physical activity for you and your family? Do you want to be healthy, but just do not have the time? You are the only person who has the power to make the time for you. You just must do it. This is the only body you have for this life of yours. I might also mention, we really, are not on this earth that long. If you are healthy, then you will have the energy to pursue those dreams of yours. It might be to travel. It might be to hike the Appalachian Trail. It might be to run a marathon. Whatever it is you dream of doing, it is easier when you are in good health.

Don't worry about what other people will say, just do it. We are all a work in progress. We all are not exactly where we want to be. Take it one day at a time. Be proud of yourself for taking that first step. I struggle every single day, just like other people do. We get wrapped up in taking care of everyone else in our world, except us. When you finally realize, you deserve to be well, then and only then, will you put yourself at the top of the list.

Chapter 9 – Talent Segmentation- Staffing

It takes a very strategic leader to see the whole picture. A lot of leaders are afraid to nurture and grow their people for fear they will be better than them. The leaders who feel this way are losing out. People follow leaders who care. People respect leaders who give of themselves unconditionally. People respect leaders who are real and see the value in their employees. Leaders who develop short term and long-term career plans for the people will build the best teams the organization has ever seen. Employees get inspired when they can see promotional opportunities in front of them. Employees get motivated on the current goals and go even farther than expected. Strategic leaders are a necessity to every organization.

These types of leaders are needed every single day. They get the job done, but as a whole team. They are great planners and have visions of seeing the end game. These types of leaders are perfect for change management and looking beyond existing programs to create better long-term sustainable organizations.

Many leaders who have this skill can see talent within the organization that can be built upon for the long-term plan. It is important to evaluate the existing talent pool and get a feel for strengths and weaknesses. Pouring continuing education into the best and most promising employees will set the stage for long term leadership down the road. Retaining current great employees is extremely important. Turnover is very costly. Employees will feel very valued and appreciated when leadership provides ample opportunities to develop short term and long-term career goals. Employees who feel this way tend to work harder, smarter, are more loyal, and are eager to share their knowledge with other new employees. It is a win-win for everyone.

Some organizations consider a forced distribution model of performance management to be an effective tool for managing talent in their organization.

A forced distribution model of performance is used to rank employees from high to low. Research has determined this attracts the type of employees who are over achievers and high talent yet have a low level of conscientiousness but high psychological entitlement (Thomason, Brownlee, Beekman Harris & Rustogi, 2018).

The two negative traits: low levels of conscientiousness and entitlement are also connected to negative outcomes in organizations. Two positive traits of this type of model are that poor performance is not tolerated at all and honesty is expected along with high performance and a culture of top talent.

I would not consider a forced distribution model because when trying to determine who the top performers are, there are many employees who are excellent employees that might just need specific educational training yet fall below the overachievers in score. These employees might be more loyal and have more defined values that are in alignment with the organization's goals and missions. Developing talent is extremely important. Sometimes, the top overachievers feel they have nothing to learn, and they are perfect, and this gives out a superior attitude which can be intimidating to others in the agency.

I would be more inclined to pair people together that can learn from each other. Also, I feel many managers do not want to have that tough discussion about poor performance, so they don't. They sometimes will document things without discussing the issues with the employees. Also, I feel giving regular feedback to employees should be ongoing and not just one time per year at the evaluation time. A lot of employees are shocked to learn their supervisors feel they are inadequate in certain areas, when they never mentioned it to the employee (Pulakos, 2004).

If an employee is ranked low on an annual evaluation, it will hurt the morale of that employee. This also filters down into the performance of that employee and possibly others. Instead, perhaps lifting that employee up with potential future educational opportunities and training that will strengthen the employee's skills and behavior.

It is important to have a solid performance management system in place that includes training and education for all staff, including top executives. A company needs to know what their talent development goals are so they can be tied into the performance review process. A company needs to also know what talent they have and where they are deficient. All talent development must tie into the organizations mission or goals. Once these are met, then an organization will understand the type of training and education that is needed to be successful (Farrell, 2012).

It is important to know where people are excelling and where they are deficient. It is also important to be open and honest with all employees about performance. If a supervisor walks around on eggshells because they don't want to hurt the employee's feelings, then the employee will never know what they need to work on to make them a better employee (Farrell, 2012).

As a whole group of employees, it will build trust and legitimacy between supervisors and employees when the truth is spoken about performance. Top performers will see their hard work is recognized and they will feel valued. Low performance employees will see what they need to work on or learn to make them better (Farrell, 2012).

Chapter 10 – The Value of Human Resources

It is important for the leader of the human resource department to be a servant and transformational leader. This job is a very demanding one because it places other's needs before their own. The director and leaders of this department must walk their talk and hold extremely high values that are instilled in the core values of the organization. The human resource department is usually the first impression of a new employee. On boarding takes place in this department. This is the perfect opportunity to share the organizational goals with the new employee. It is the perfect opportunity to tie the employee's daily work to the organizational goals, which inspires employees to work together as teams and strive for excellence (Bachelder, 2018).

The leaders of the human resource department must be very humble and hold themselves accountable. This department usually handles problems such as employee grievances, labor disputes, financial garnishments, employee assistance, payroll, compensation, and training. This department looks at every job description and is responsible for evaluating them every year. Everything changes, including individual job descriptions. With this, comes adjustments in pay grade, evaluations, career development goals, and recruitment. When evaluating the future goals of an organization, the leaders of HR will be the people who decide if new positions should be created and their purpose.

This department sees everything that is going on in the organization. They have a finger on the pulse of the employees and know usually ahead of time if employees are not happy. This department is the place to go if you, yourself, do not know how to handle a situation or even a toxic employee. Human Resource employees are talented, skilled, smart, and will give the correct advice in any given situation. If they do not know the answer, they are not afraid to say so. They will ensure they have the correct advice from the correct source.

The employee assistance programs are usually under this department. As leadership changes, so must the employee assistance programs. Most organizations are operating in the leadership mindset of the early nineteen-seventies. It is time, to upgrade all departments, and especially, the organization's employee assistance programs. I say this, not because the topics of need have changed, but the methods of coping have advanced, and solutions to problems have changed. People will always have problems with finances, food, aging parents, death of loved ones, addiction of some sort, divorce, abuse, or mental health. It is the future of wellness in the workplace, to help people find easier solutions of coping. It is about paying attention. It is time to pay attention and serve the people of the organization.

It is a great idea for the HR department to invite employee participation when it comes to upgrading the new employee assistance program. There may be ideas or suggestions that other people have not considered.

Healthy and happy employees lower turnover rates, increase productivity, loyalty, longevity, and customer satisfaction.

The key functions of Human Resources are to handle all employment policies for the agency which includes compensation and benefits, health and safety, communications, and compliance with the Fair Labor Standards Act, Occupational Health and Safety Agencies, and the anti-discrimination and sexual harassment employment laws (Turban, Pollard & Wood, 2017).

The Anti-discrimination Employment Laws are as follows:

Title VII of the Civil Rights Act of 1964 – This law "prohibits discrimination based on race, color, religion, national origin, and sex. It also prohibits sex discrimination based on pregnancy and sexual harassment" (Turban, Pollard & Wood, 2017).

The Civil Rights Act of 1966 – This law "prohibits discrimination based on sex or ethnic origin" (Turban, Pollard & Wood, 2017).

Equal Pay Act of 1963 – "Prohibits employers from paying different wages to men and women who perform essentially the same work under similar working conditions" (Turban, Pollard & Wood, 2017).

Bankruptcy Act – Prohibits discrimination against anyone who has filed bankruptcy.

Americans With Disabilities Act – Prohibits discrimination against anyone that has a disability.

Equal Employment Opportunity Act – This law prohibits discrimination against minorities that have a poor credit rating.

Age Discrimination Act- This law prohibits discrimination against anyone who is over forty years old (Turban, Pollard & Wood, 2017).

This is a lot of responsibility for any organization, and it helps if the organization does have a human resource department to handle all of this. Many organizations are so large, they are moving the human resource information system to the cloud or intranet.

One large benefit of moving the human resource information system to intranets or the cloud is that it takes the physical workload from employees and opens the door for employees to manage their own information through a system. Taking the mundane tasks like changing direct deposit information or adding family members to a health insurance policy away from the human resource department employees, frees those employees to focus on compliance of all the laws noted above. It also gives the HR department more time to recruit and to train new employees.

Management, recruitment, and development, include employee service evaluations and developing existing employees to prepare them for promotions or more advanced positions within the agency.

Many organizations have concerns about implementing Saas HR (software as a service). All the information that is retained regarding employees must be stored and this affects the agency as far as protecting the privacy of the employee and their personnel records. The agency must conform to federal laws regarding Drug Free Workplace and in some instances, agencies have been sued by employees for unlawful searches and wrongful discharge, etc. The Employment Laws require the agency to protect the employee private information.

The cost of recruitment of new employees is high. There are many ways to help reduce this cost. They can use social media to recruit, such as LinkedIn or Facebook. More than 90% of corporations use LinkedIn for recruitment purposes (Turban, Pollard & Wood, 2017). This can cut the time it takes to recruit and to sort through thousands of resumes to find the right person. On LinkedIn, certain words can be added that describe the job and the qualifications which can eliminate a lot of time it takes to answer questions about the position.

The Information Technology department is very important for human resource planning and control. The IT department is necessary because when it comes to control and planning, protecting the agency and the agency's integrity is important. For example, if there is only one person that is authorized to cut a check to a company for purchasing supplies, if there isn't a control in place to oversee this, the person can have a check cut to an old buddy he/she went to school with, and it might be for more than what the supplies are worth. It protects fraud from happening. An IT manager or someone in the Finance and Accounting department can implement policy that requires all checks to be signed by two people, or to be approved by someone other than the person authorizing the check. The protocols are important for everyone as it protects the agency and the employees from being part of fraud.

In today's market, all corporations must be on top of their game and that includes having an efficient and smooth-running HR department. The information technology software and hardware that can be invested in by an agency, can not only store large amounts of data, but can manipulate, communicate, and record data across all geographical areas around the world. Information can be tracked, and it can also help in making important decisions. There are at least two kinds of expert system applications that corporations can use to sort data and make decisions. Black box system will give a recommendation outcome without telling the user how it came to that conclusion (Broderick & Boudreau, 1992). Another kind is the training system which when implemented, can ask the user questions, and provides information as to why the decision might be what it is. However, this information was from a 1992 reference and as fast as technology changes, there are many more expert systems on the market that can take a corporation to the front when it comes to managing the HR department.

Managers face huge challenges to stay in the front runner but also corporations need to think about investments in information technology that not only helps them meet the global challenges in business, but to move them far ahead of everyone else.

Chapter 11 – Human Resources and Job Descriptions

Job descriptions are required by the Department of Labor (VERBONCU & ZEININGER, 2015). They were originally created to hold people accountable for the duties and used in disciplinary actions if someone failed to do their job. However, over the past decade, Job Descriptions have become more of a HR managerial tool. The HR departments are responsible for creating the job descriptions and setting the salary or wage to each job. Times are changing and more companies are going towards a whole team concept. This is where a team works together to make sure its department meets its goals and responsibilities, together.

All companies have job descriptions, and these have served as a basis of structure to ensure output is accomplished. When a manager can establish objectives in a department, it helps forecast the future outcome. Setting tasks develops structure within an organization or department. When an employee or team can come together and negotiate tasks to get the job done, this empowers the whole team and motivates them (VERBONCU & ZEININGER, 2015).

More companies are giving more authority to employees, so they are held accountable and responsible for their tasks. This also empowers them to be better and become more productive. The purpose of an HR manager is to attract the right people to the job, hire them, educate them, train, motivate, empower, and reward them.

Everything is constantly changing at a fast pace, and this affects the business world, as well. These changes affect workplaces as well. We see responsibility differently. We hold people accountable differently. Also, with the world and global enterprise, different people around the world are interacting differently (Strycharczyk & Elvin, 2014 Strycharczyk, D., & Elvin, C. (2014). Although many companies are entering new markets around the world, there are just as many who are not global. These companies do not have a global mindset and maybe they should have a global mindset.

As an HR leader, it is their responsibility to see the big picture and embrace and trust the complete understanding of ethics and ethical behavior. We need to understand what is ahead in the future with technology and how we can utilize new technology to advance our companies well ahead of others in the industry. Companies are becoming more creative and capturing the creativity of teams in departments. Job Descriptions, I feel will always remain as a basis, but the need to come together and work together to empower together is what creates strong companies.

Job descriptions are designed to ensure goals and tasks are completed. Job descriptions will always need to be changed and updated by expert personnel and managers; however, they are a very useful management tool.

Chapter 12 – Human Resource Challenges

Three challenges in HR include global diversity in the workplace, human capital, and management. I believe management is the most critical for HR to address. This is the first time in history where there are five generations of people working. Every generation was raised differently. Every generation has different values and goals. The older generation can't afford to retire just yet, and most are set in their ways and do not have the skills or desire to learn anything related to the digital age. These older managers look at things differently, especially how they manage people. A lot of these types are still operating within the good ole boy system. Many leaders or managers who have been in the positions for a long time are afraid of change. They are afraid of losing their jobs to a younger person. They also, at some time, might have been top of their game, but as years go by and competition steps in, it is even harder to keep the status quo, let alone, embrace change, and try to find ways to pull the business out of a natural decline.

Sometimes, leadership can be part of the problem (Schultz & Walt, 2015). It is difficult for declining companies to adapt to changes and reinvent themselves. When shareholders and upper managers meet only once per year, employees will always be in the dark. They will never know if they are going to be working the next month or not. They can be truly paralyzed with fear of losing their jobs and income. This only adds to the crisis because people who are constantly worried about their jobs will not engage with customers and others and eventually have overall performance decrease (Schultz & Walt, 2015). Also, when management does not share information with employees, the employees do not have any idea what the strategic goals and missions are for the organization. It is difficult to align yourself if you do not know what to align to. Many organizations have a difficult time with embracing changes because this means old traditions must be challenged also (Horst & Järventie-Thesleff, 2016).

There are many things that need to take place to get an organization back on track. There are five steps that must take place: You must identify the differences between the corporate strategy and the current critical tasks at hand. You must identify the former culture, the current environmental, operational environment, relationships and their effectiveness and efficiency. You must examine every aspect of the business and improve on every aspect of it. You must change the culture, organization, and people by implementing corrective action steps that need to take place. And lastly, you must implement new changes to make sure corporate strategy and all people and departments are on the same page.

It takes time to implement change. In this case, it would probably take two or three years to see a big difference. The HR department will play a huge role in this massive change that is needed. Several things that HR can do to help pave the way for transformational changes is to share communication with everyone. This can be by email, phone, meetings, etc. (Schultz & Walt, 2015) They also need to have a big message and share it with a sense of urgency and empowerment. They can include the employees as part of the changes. This will make the employees feel important and needed. It might also reassure them about their job status (Schultz & Walt, 2015).

As these newer generations are merging with the older generations, building teams, and pairing younger people with the older people can be very transformational. The older ones share so much wisdom about the history of the company and the way things used to be. The younger ones can share more technology and things connected to the digital age to make jobs easier. Things that used to be done by hand and took months to prepare, might only take a few strokes of a key on a computer to generate the same data.

HR is changing, and more and more broader responsibilities are being added to this department. A lot of corporations rely on the HR department for guidance during massive changes. It is the leader's responsibility to ensure your HR leaders are top notch. It is also critical this department has the staff and tools they need to perform efficiently.

Chapter 13 – Human Resources- Training & Development

It is critical to any organization that all employees stay motivated and committed to the mission and goals established. It is also very important every organization knows who their best employee is and who has potential for improvement. Corporations must always be forward thinking and looking for top employees to fill positions that may come available in the future.

Many organizations fill top positions through recommendations of supervisors or by employee evaluations. However, to be effective in retaining top employees and employees that hold very positive potential, it is essential organizations create a training program specifically tailored to the business it offers. To limit resentment from some staff, it is imperative management cite the requirements for the training program to all staff. Also, advise staff that the opportunity will be available to all employees at a future date (Edwards, 2012).

Training and development of employees will be an expensive investment, but one that will pay in return, tenfold. All educational opportunities should be aligned with the corporate objectives that all staff can understand. It is important to identify all training needs within an organization. In order to obtain this information, every department head could be on a task force to identify training skills and talent needed to perform every job in the individual departments.

Once training objectives are identified, it is important for managers to ascertain the openness of employees to the thought of new training, training styles, and training design. A decision must be made whether to outsource training or to develop onsite training with trained professionals inside the organization. Prior to educational training being delivered, it is also important to have a plan. A plan for regular onsite training and a plan for advanced learning for key employees. Having a plan in place and employees trained for jobs in the future helps organizations adapt when a crisis arises that is unexpected.

There are many performance gaps in many different agencies. One of the biggest performance gaps is identifying and training employees to learn and be prepared for promotions in supervisory and management roles. A training program can ensure top employees are ready when a vacancy occurs in the future.

It is important that every agency have a culture of learning and working together. The first step in any organization is to have a very supportive learning environment. An employee feels supported by management when he/she can share new ideas and feel free to utilize their talents to perform a job (DeMotta, Gonzales & Lawson, 2019). If an employee makes an error, they can feel safe to ask questions, to correct those errors in performance. Employees feel empowered when they are encouraged to take risks and explore new opportunities to design or implement new products or procedures that will make the company successful.

In designing a training program to train top employees for future management positions, it is critical to inspire open dialogue between employees and management. Managers should encourage and collaborate, to create a teamwork environment towards training. Managers can create a knowledge baseline and be open to innovation from employees. Managers need to value their employee's ideas and thoughts to create a bond of trust between staff and employees.

A strategic HRD approach to design and delivery will include workforce competence and the employee skill development for the jobs at hand. Preparing employees to respond to many different types of changes that can happen in an organization, will also teach employees how to appreciate educational opportunities of all kinds.

Many organizations can use the social learning approach to training and delivery of their employees. This can also be incorporated when preparing those top employees for future advancement. The social learning theory is applied when employees are mentored by superiors to learn their jobs. Learning by experiencing and watching others is widely accepted practice in many organizations.

I would recommend a leadership mentoring program. This would include partnering with local universities and creating a top-of-the-line leadership program that would be tailored to the organization at hand. The training program would include diversity in the workplace, global business environment, along with human resource practices and labor laws. The HR department could also create online training programs that are easily accessible, and can be completed after hours, for training credits. Other training seminars could be locked in at certain times of the year when times are slower, and employees have the time to be away from the office.

Leadership mentoring program will include senior level managers. These senior staff will ensure employees understand their commitment to a culture of leadership training. As top employees are mentored by senior staff, they will learn more of the bigger picture of the organization. This will ensure they are more prepared to step up when they are needed in emergencies, or as a promotion. Topics on mental health issues can also be included. Employee resources can be made available to all level of employees that could include topics such as financial planning, alcohol and substance abuse programs, smoking cessation classes, along with stress management training (Dimoff, & Kelloway, 2019).

It is important for any agency to conduct a survey to determine what training and development is lacking in the organization. Identifying all the current training and enhancing it to make it better, is also important. Organizations can create policy and procedures to ensure training and development is mandatory for all employees. Requiring employees to obtain a certain number of credits each year will enrich the employee's knowledge substantially. Develop training specifically to retain those employees that are considered top talent, is crucial.

Creating educational development that teaches staff how to communicate effectively, delegate and how to become a coach themselves, will strengthen the organization. Ensuring senior staff personally get involved in leadership training will send a strong message of a supportive leadership culture (DeMotta, Gonzales & Lawson, 2019.

The results of implementing a new leadership training and development program can be measured through surveys of staff and senior management. This can encourage training designs to be constantly improving. If an organization sets up new policy and procedures that make training and development mandatory to all staff, measures can be taken to ensure those are adhered to, and to ensure those lacking can be scheduled. Measurements can be made in performance improvement and production if those types of statistics are made available.

Measurements can also be taken through employee evaluations. Establishing job responsibilities and duties and ensuring the management have an ongoing feedback program, creates an open communication between staff and senior management. This also can help employees learn throughout the year, and not only on the annual evaluation. Adding leadership development training programs to any agency will ensure thriving commitment and innovation from employees to stay for the long term.

Chapter 14 – Best Practices - International Human Resources

International Human Resource Management (IHRM) is the management of all human resources in the global environment for organizations who are multinational, successful, and want to have the competitive advantage within the market (Zheng, 2016). Human Resource Management activities in the domestic scene include organizational planning, staffing, benefits, recruiting, training, diversity, ethics, and managing employee development. While the IHRM includes all of these, it goes far beyond, to include the transferring of knowledge as it relates to each individual country, along with how to manage cultural diversity.

Success in the global environment is influenced by the many different cultural settings and environments. In years past, the focus has been on attitudes, staffing, and expatriates. In most recent times, the focus has improved to dive deeper into the expatriate management. This has included individual skills and attributes and how they relate to the team behavior as well as how successful the individual is in building strong friendships in the cultural setting (Zheng, 2016). Building strong friendships in different cultures enhances work performance and strengthens expatriate commitment.

The global environment continues to change as the aging workforce declines and creates a significant talent shortage around the world. Many organizations recognize the importance to include gender diversity along with cultural diversity in their workplace. It is important to become strategic when focusing on talent management in the global setting. It has become even more important for organizations to develop a plan to recruit top talent, as well as retain top talent if they want to keep a competitive advantage. What separates the past from the present in managing diverse talent is not just managing the skills of the diverse workforce, but managing the different values the diverse workforce brings to the table.

When organizations are committed to teaching each other, language barriers and cultural diversity also becomes a focus of importance. Sometimes, it is better to form a partnership and alliance than to start from scratch. People from different cultures process information differently. For this reason, it can be helpful for organizations to create a team of experts that cover legal, financial, marketing, technology, lab, and operations. Both sides can visit each other's headquarters and conduct feasibility studies. When ready, the organizations can agree on partnership terms.

It is extremely important organizations demonstrate strong leadership commitment to partnerships. Without strong leadership commitment and focus, the partnership might not be successful. Both parties should focus on building strong interpersonal relationships with each other and recruiting top talent that is bilingual in both English and the country's host language. This will eliminate a lot of the language and culture barriers that might exist. In addition, a reward system for learning can be highly effective. Organizations can both recruit not only bilingual potential employees, but potential employees that display strong leadership capabilities with a global mindset (Zheng, 2016).

Most Asian countries have not developed their expatriate programs. When they send someone out of their country, the employee is not promised any position upon return. Most employees accept they will return to their former position (Kang & Shen, 2013). Although, many companies feel working overseas gives an employee a competitive edge, they also feel it is good for employee career development. Many countries realize they do not pay enough attention to employee career development and repatriation issues such as readjustments and family issues. This only serves to increase the high repatriate turnover within the organization.

It is important for organizations to recognize the barriers that exist when doing business around the globe. Many companies develop strategic plans to ensure the exchange of information is successful between countries. This can include recruiting and hiring potential applicants that display leadership qualities and a global mindset. These top applicants should be able to speak both languages as this helps eliminate many cultural and language barriers that might otherwise exist between them. In addition, success becomes easier to grasp when both parties acknowledge their lack of skills and their strengths. This opens the door for each side to eagerly learn from each other. One of the most important facets that stands out when looking at two organizations from different countries, is the ability to be open minded and work together. They should appreciate and respect each other's knowledge and skills. It is also beneficial if they embrace each other's culture and language. They can develop a cultural learning system that will enable everyone to be on the same page, with the same information, at all times.

To encourage this style of learning, employees can be assigned short term assignments that include training and development of specific jobs. Employees can relocate not only between jobs, but between countries to encourage cross training and retention of all kinds of knowledge. Establishing a reward system for learning motivates employees to expand and develop their personal selves.

In considering an international assignment, one of the most important things to look at is the human resource training and development the company has created. This will tell a lot about an organization and how they value their employees, not just for the short term, but the long-term investment. To ensure a lower employee turnover rate, more attention should be focused on employee's career development and placement upon returning to their own country. Organizations with strong expatriate programs provide counseling to assist families with cultural and language barrier issues along with career development after an assignment has been completed (Kang & Shen, 2013).

The things that are most important for international human resource management departments to remember, is to value the cultural differences of the top talent recruited, along with the diverse skills they bring with them. It is critical for an organization to create a global mindset among all staff that includes the strengths and weakness of everyone involved. This opens the door to motivating employees to learn new things. It also helps build strong interpersonal relationships and strong leadership in all countries working together (Thite, et al, 2014).

Chapter 15 – Primary Aspects of International HR

The primary aspects of an effective International Human Resource Management Program are to ensure employees are well trained in the diversity and culture of the country they are traveling to, and to ensure their families have the proper knowledge of that country. When an employee's tour is concluded, there should also be a program to help that person re-enter the USA with the skills and knowledge of how to fit back in. This might be a gradual transition because if a person has been in a country, say for five years, performing a specific task related to that country, they have developed a skill that could possibly be used when they return. For example, they could share their experience with people who are being prepared to go to other countries.

Many people come back and find they do not fit in anywhere because the skills they learned are not needed here. The IHRM program should provide the employee with a list of jobs they could come back to because of their skill level. Developing employees should be a priority in the international human resource management program. Employees who agree to go overseas, should get credit and preference for jobs when they return because of this (Kang & Shen, 2013).

In addition, the IHRM program should ensure that housing, travel, food, utilities, vaccinations, etc. are taken care of prior to the employee leaving the USA. Everything should be made easy for the employee. The program should also provide a twenty-four-hour hotline number to the employee in case of emergency. When a person comes home, he and his family, if he has one, should be required to attend some type of counseling session to prepare them. Employees can be frustrated and even disheartened when they return and must take a job that is beneath them when they have been trained for so much more. The IHRM program should ensure they feel appreciated and accepted back home when they return.

Many times, corporate polices, rules, employee handbooks, etc. must be modified to the country the person is going to be working in. For example, it is illegal to put a nine-year old to work full time, yet Africa abuses the child labor laws. Just because it is an accepted practice, I feel it is critical the person working in that country pay attention to the international laws also as a guideline. An employee working in another country for their corporation should know they are representing their corporation and they should have firm ethical values. Also, the person needs to know what the employee standards are for that country. They might not allow a woman to talk to a group of men, where in the USA, it is common to have female leaders. Another example, is IHRM should inform the employee what the taxation laws are for that country and how contracts are negotiated, etc. (Brisco, Schuler & Claus, 2009).

There are so many different aspects of the IHRM program that should be included. If a person agrees to go overseas and does not take his/her family, this can create a hardship on both husband-and-wife side. They might have to pay for housing at both locations, causing a hardship. Also, time apart can be difficult. If an employee takes the whole family, it will require the whole family to adjust to everything, including behavior that is expected from that country (Bartram & Dowling, 2013).

It would be nice if before a person agrees to leave the USA, the corporation offer them a solid position in writing prior to that person leaving. This way, the employee knows after they do their tour of duty, they have something solid to come back to, not just a promise.

Another area that I would consider to be important, is if a person is going to be a leader or manager in another country, they need to understand the protocol for recognition and disciplinary actions. In some countries, the people work as a team, and it is not about just one person. If a manager singles out just one person because they see that person working hard on a project and they leave out the entire team, it can cause problems.

Chapter 16 – Expatriate Recruitment

Many countries are considered to still be underdeveloped. In cases such as these, it is even more important for the human resource manager to research the political environment, culture of the people, business practices along with labor laws and job requirements. It is helpful if someone can speak the language and know the culture and environment. Many times, problems occur when an expatriate does not meet the job requirements and cannot adjust to the environment (Dordevic, 2016).

It is a competitive business, and it is becoming even more difficult to recruit top talent. There are three different approaches to recruiting: ethnocentric, polycentric, and geocentric (Dordevic, 2016). Ethnocentric is comparing one culture with your own. For example, the way a person eats. In Asia, many eat with chopsticks and in the remote parts of Asia, they might not even have forks or spoons. It is important to know the differences. The polycentric approach is where the nationals of the host country are hired to be the managers and handle the responsibility of duties for the subsidiary company. The geocentric is where the right person for the job is hired no matter where they are from around the globe.

In looking to recruit expatriates, many already have the culture experience needed so it is important to make sure the job skills and knowledge are present also. One important factor to consider when hiring expatriates, is whether the person is like the environment they are going to be working in. For example, ethnicity, someone that might be from that country would be trusted more and quicker than someone who is a total opposite and brand new that has to build and develop the trust of the locals (Fan, et al, 2018). This would be an advantage of hiring a local to manage the job.

Locals in the community might not embrace someone from another country as well as they would from one of their own. This can cause barriers to communication. It also can create sabotage to a project if the locals are resentful of the outsider. They might withhold information or make things harder than need be. This is especially true in India or China (Fan, et al, 2018). Both locals and the expatriates need to trust each other, so the burden is on both sides. Many locals might feel outsiders are taking jobs that should belong to them. In some countries, there might even be violence because of this.

When selecting an expatriate for a job, it is important there is a plan to train, educate, prepare, and culturally adapt that person to the upcoming environment. Many failures are caused by the lack of information sharing between the organization and the expatriate (Haile & White, 2019).

Even after an expatriate is chosen and sent overseas, the training should be continuous. There should be a strong support system for the expatriate and his/her family in both locations. The culture, language and day to day matters are extremely important. For example, a person needs to know where to go and what to do in case of a health crisis. The goal is to have a positive experience and create a good impact with the employee and their skills and knowledge for the future.

In summary, it is important to consider a person's past history, family situation, ethnicity, gender, age, skills, knowledge, languages, as well as a person's mental state, when recruiting expatriates for a job (Kandogan, 2018). I would believe all of these are vitally important. It does help if a person can speak the language and has some experience in that country. It also could be to the advantage to hire both expatriate and a local as managers to work together.

Chapter 17 – Build or Buy Talent

Human resource managers have many decisions to make that affect their company. Among those decisions, is to decide whether to build upon the current staff or to buy talent for specific jobs. It is essential the jobs required get done well. Both choices can be challenging to a human resource manager but also rewarding. Markets have demanded many changes over the past decade and organizational needs must adjust.

Many organizations over the past twenty years have downsized or had a need to cut costs in order to stay in business. Many of these firms have changed permanent employees to non-permanent employees. Reaching out to buy talent can be very effective, whether it is for low skilled labor or specialized skills.

Designing and creating a solid and empowered company can begin with investing in its own employees. Many employees see their jobs evolving into more than they were when they were hired. Organizations that invest in continuing education and training for staff members can see a powerful shift in productivity and loyalty.

Buying talent or building on the talents of current employees is a common choice human resource managers make every day. Both options depend upon organizational needs and time.

Global markets have changed over the past several decades and keep changing. This requires organizations to become flexible during times of expansions or contraction. A company can hire someone that is not a permanent employee but a sub-contractor or independent contractor. Many firms choose this route because it does not require a long- term commitment and it also can bring innovation from the contractors who are not influenced by the internal culture. Hiring from outside of an organization is called externalization (Finch, Hillenbrand, O'Reilly, & Varella, 2015).

When an organization hires independents from the outside, this opens whole new diversified fields. These fields can include seasonal workers, for example, that might take care of landscaping and lawn care. It also could include temporary people to help with holiday seasons, for example, in sales during Christmas or Thanksgiving season. If a permanent worker takes leave due to the Family Leave Act, a company might hire a temporary independent worker to fill the space until that permanent employee comes back to work. Many companies hire special skilled consultants to come in and perform audits or perhaps design a new building on the premises.

Some organizations who are opening new markets in other countries can hire independent contractors or specialists to scout out the potential in those countries prior to investment decisions. The advantages of hiring independent workers and specialists are many. When a company hires someone from the outside in this status, there is most always a contract. This contract binds the contractor to the agency until the job is done. It will specify the job to be done and the amount to be paid. Most of the time, it will also cite a deadline for the job to be done. When both parties review and sign the contract, it is binding to both parties. When the job is done, the contractor moves on to his next job and the liability of the company is over (Finch, Hillenbrand, O'Reilly & Varella, 2015).

There are owners of large, and many times, multiple corporations globally. These owners want to improve the existing companies and they might hire outside executives to evaluate and report on those companies. Many companies also are in the business of buying out other companies. In these circumstances, the companies do not have time to recruit for top leaders. Instead, they find resources that hire top leading executives to step in and take charge with little notice (Crockett & McGregor, 2007).

Buying labor also has its weaknesses. Many contractors have a high turnover rate because they pay low wages to their staff and the jobs might be seasonal or far and few between. Some contractors do not require background checks on their employees because they know they will only be around for a short period of time. Because of the non- background checks, often the workers hired by the contractor have a history of theft, terminations, incarceration, and possibly drug use. These people might be hard workers for a short period of time, but they also might be a threat at the job site to an agency, depending on the agency.

Higher payments for contract labor are normal. However, in the long scheme of things, the agency does not have to pay health benefits, vacation or sick leave, or retirement. Paying higher wages might be hard on a small company and a disadvantage but would be considered an advantage by a larger company.

Challenges for management or human resource departments happen because they do not have any control over contract laborers. An independent contractor is considered a person who has control of how he does a job and when he does a job. If a human resource manager has a problem with an independent contractor or one of their employees, the most they can do is talk to the independent contractor. The independent contractor is not bound by any corporation employee handbook rules or policy. They are their own boss. Their commitment is to the contract they signed for a specific job and when that is complete, the job is done.

Long-term advantages of contract labor are a company builds a relationship with that person. These relationships also go both ways. The contractor might refer the company to another company for future business, or the company might refer the contractor to another company for more work. Contract laborers are not eligible for benefits and are responsible for any injuries while on a job site (Morgan, 2018). Many companies like independent contractors for this reason. It saves the company a lot of money every year.

A disadvantage of being a contract laborer, is they are not protected by federal or state employment laws. If there is a problem, the contract laborer might have to sue in small claims court or civil court to find resolution. Another disadvantage of hiring contract labor, is if a company does not understand the laws surrounding contract labor, and they treat the person as an employee by telling them what to do, when to do it, and how to do it, etc., they open the door for the IRS to audit. This could potentially become a tax evasion charge if the company is using contract labor for regular employee positions (Morgan, 2018).

Many times, managers misclassify staff because of how they interpret the laws, and not for financial gain. If an employee is properly classified as a permanent employee and not an independent contractor, everything should be well. However, if a permanent employee is classified as an independent contractor, the agency could be open to civil penalties along with failure to pay employee withholding taxes along with matching funds to the IRS (Morgan, 2018). If there are more than one person misclassified, the company could be open to a Class Action lawsuit.

Building talent is a priority by all types of companies and organizations from non-profit, small business, large corporations, private and public around the world. Agencies are investing in their own people to create a talent driven culture that produces fantastic results. IBM and Western Union are in the top five in the globe for investing in their employees, to create a better company (Building talent, 2017).

Many companies are already planning for beyond 2022. As the digital age advances even farther those expectations, it is critical to ensure employees have the necessary skills and talent to keep up with the changes. Everything is changing, including the way employees connect with others. Social media is being used by companies, and this requires new communication skills for employees. The younger generation are usually very adept at digital devices, but they are not the only employees. Employees range through five generations. It is essential companies invest in easy-to-understand training for employees to bring everyone up to par (KIDANU, 2018).

There is a huge need to develop employees for upcoming new industry, new commerce, and new technology. Companies are embracing team concepts that require employees to be creative and innovative thinkers. It is important employees are educated on diversity and culture values, so they can work in international or global environments (KIDANU, 2018).

The advantages of investing in employees are many. Employees stay with companies who show they care about them. Companies that pay good wages and benefits and keep up with the changing economy by investing in education for their staff, will have higher productivity and loyalty. One disadvantage of investing in employees might be to lose a few to the competition. Sometimes employees who receive certifications or advanced education might decide to change career fields because they now qualify. There will always be some who leave, but the majority will stay.

An employee is a person that is hired by a company as a permanent or part time staff member. The company pays wages and are held accountable to the federal and state employment laws including wages, unemployment, and workers compensation. Employees are the biggest resource a company has. Human resource managers must manage the talent of all employees, so people are utilizing their best skills and assets for the company. Globalization and opening of new markets have forced companies to ensure all employees are trained and educated in political, culture, diversity, economic, and technological environments (King & Vaiman, 2019).

Advantages of investing in employees comes with employees becoming more engaged with organizations and more trusting. Employees tend to stay with companies who spend money on them. Educating employees also makes the employee more mobile and deployable if needed. Management also becomes more involved with employees and can create a performance management system (King & Vaiman, 2019). This also supports forward movement within a company.

Employees have a set of mental and social skills that allow them to display their best work. Employers can manage this by coaching and educating employees to develop talent. Employees respond, by having a sense of belonging and greater confidence. Teaching employees advanced skills demonstrates a trust the employer has in an employee. It also creates mentors in an organization, where new employees can be partnered with, to learn (Subotnik, 2015).

Disadvantages of NOT investing in employees include high turnover rate, low employee satisfaction rates, and low productivity. There is always the chance an employee will move on after a company has invested a lot of money into them. This is a risk that is worth taking.

Human resource managers have tough choices when it comes to hiring labor. Buying talent works well for seasonal labor or special projects, etc. Independent contractors are those who are free from the control of the agency that hired them, have their own business in the type of work that is required, and the work that the contractor performs is different than the work the agency provides. Hiring talent is a legitimate business practice and has been around for a long time.

Investing in employees can sometimes be expensive, however, many companies are moving into new markets and globalization and the demand requires all employees be educated to effectively and successfully work in different cultures and environments. Investing in employees helps corporations move into the future and stay ahead of competition. This can also be a challenge for human resource managers. The responsibility to keep up with training and education can be a full-time job.

I would be encouraged to build on the employees in an organization. It would be great to have a reputation within the community or globally that people want to work for the company. It says a lot about how the company treats its employees. When choosing what type of talent to hire, it is important to consider long term goals, where the company is heading, and what the current needs are. If the hiring manager is well educated in the laws of contract labor and such, the decision should be an easy one to make.

Chapter 18 – Compensation/Performance Reviews

During the financial crisis many people were outraged at the amount of pay CEOs were receiving in many large corporations. Companies were laying off thousands of employees while CEOs were getting huge ridiculous bonuses at the end of the year.

Many organizations hire CEO's without knowing their ability to perform, so the contracts are based on time periods. For example, the first year might specifically pay $150,000. The second-year pay will be based upon the success of the first year including profits and business conditions (Chaigneau & Sahuguet, 2018). The end of the second year, the firm or agency will have a firm belief about the hired CEO's capabilities. If the belief is low, then they usually terminate the contract with the CEO. If the belief is high, then the organization might settle in for a long-term contract with stock options and other benefits.

The Omnibus Budget Reconciliation Act (OBRA) of 1993 went into effect Jan. 1, 1994. This legislation capped the corporation's tax deductible, to one million dollars per CEO, unless it qualified for performance-based pay (Blackwell, Dudney & Farrell, 2007). There is a lot of research that shows the OBRA did not have much effect on large firms, because the companies just restructured their CEO contracts, to be more performance based.

Many companies have increased stock grants, based upon performance, and these incentives appear to be so valuable the CEO's performances have increased at most large firms. In companies where unions have organized, the CEO's compensation is more controlled and substantially less than those firms that do not have a union (Huang, Jiang, Lie & Que, 2017). However, unions do pay attention to what the CEO's make, and often use this as a negotiation tactic, and the firms count on it. It is believed that lower CEO pay can strengthen the bargaining power, and spreads good will between the CEO's and with unions, and other parties. Many CEOs of these type of firms work hard because they know their pay is based on the quality of work they provide, and they can be replaced easily.

There are other alternatives that work better for long term organizational growth and profitability.

Many CEOs are paid higher salaries because their contracts are based on high risk. The high-risk pay is contingent on the CEO performing criteria that is not known in the future. In today's business world, many CEOs are paid higher because of their experience in global enterprise and international trade, etc. Many compensation packages are complex and are tailored to fit the company itself. Still, there is a large inequity regarding CEO compensation around the world. Because many compensation packages are performance based, they also hinge on the market during that time (Conyan, 2018). Many companies today are offering stock options even to low level employees as an incentive to motivate them and retain good employee's long term. If profits increase and employees receive benefits financially from this, it seems it would change behaviors of all employees to become better performers.

HR managers could also establish pay grades for all employees, including unclassified or contract CEO's. This would establish a guaranteed pay and help firms plan their financial goals for the future knowing what their costs would be for long term. Many companies are also giving perks like memberships to physical fitness companies and golf memberships at country clubs. These types of perks add up and are attractive, especially when given with stock options for the company.

I feel a CEO should be paid well for a job well done. Many firms hire different types of CEO's based on the type of firms there are. And most CEO's have worked years to get where they are. I do feel firms should pay their employees well if they want to retain them, but also, there needs to be a difference in salary between the CEO and the employees that have low levels of responsibility. I also believe when a company offers stock to a CEO, it behooves the CEO to work hard to make the company a success. Then everyone wins.

Organizations that conduct research outside of their facility, to ensure their internal pay for performance rates are fair and accurate, will have less employee lawsuits and more satisfied employees. To be successful in the pay for performance market, it requires regular updates to job descriptions, upper management support, employee trust, a solid merit system that rewards exceptional employees, and a flexible compensation plan (Koss, 2008).

In Oklahoma, state agencies have been around for over a hundred years. Over the past thirty years, the organizations have become more compliant with federal and state laws relating to employment governance. Many employees that make it past the five years of service are rewarded with opportunities for advancement into management, along with pay bonuses directly related to performance and years of service.

The Personnel departments review all the job descriptions within the individual agencies every year to ensure the pay is fair and equitable with other states. This ensures employees do not have a legal grievance towards the agency, and they know they are being treated fairly and with respect. The agency is required to have an affirmative action plan. The agencies have regular employee evaluations that provides the employee with a set of goals and rewards the employee with a merit system compensation pay increase. When supervisors and managers provide timely and accurate evaluations, it builds trust between employees and management. The employees know they are being dealt with fairly and within the expected time frame.

The State of Oklahoma does not look for the lowest paid employee. They are always searching for top notch potential employees who demonstrate loyalty to their current employer and are looking for an organization that pays well for performance given. The agency also does not just give pay increases to those employees once a year. It evaluates employees of all departments and rewards employees for exceptional service. This also sets a standard for the agency, and all those who join the agency know and understand the commitment that management has towards rewarding its people for a job well done.

In the State of Oklahoma, all state agencies receive an annual cost of living adjustment (COLA) when approved by the Governor. Anyone who is a permanent employee and on the current merit system step pay compensation, will receive an annual COLA along with their pay for performance increase. There have been times, in past years, where cost of living adjustments and hiring freezes were in place. Another challenge of the pay for performance, is there is a cap. Many employees who have worked for fifteen to twenty years or so have reached the top of the pay scale, and there is nowhere to go after that, unless they change jobs or positions with higher pay. This can be disheartening also for correctional officers and probation and parole officers. Once they reach the highest class, that is it. They might work another ten years or so without a performance pay increase, only a COLA. However, in Oklahoma, they have established the twenty-year retirement plan for law enforcement officers.

When an agency has good managers and supervisors who are on top of their evaluations and employee development, employees are very happy. Sometimes, there are managers who are not good at their job, and this filters down to the subordinates below them. Sometimes, employees suffer without pay performance increases solely because they have ineffective managers above them. It is a process for large organizations with thousands of employees to continuously evaluate their managers and cut loose those who do not support the mission and goals of the agency.

It would be my recommendation to budget every year for COLA for all employees. The money could be generated from other resources, and this would go a long way to keep employees happy and doing a good job. Compensation is not just about getting paid for a job done. It is about everything including the working environment, happiness on the job, safety on the job, educational opportunities, and promotional opportunities along with benefits such as vacation, sick leave, and health insurance (Koss, 2008).

The State of Oklahoma does a great job in reviewing the annual job descriptions and employee evaluations. Most supervisors are very good with making sure employees are evaluated on time. The IT department provides a monthly printout of all employees who are due for evaluations. The agency also has a process in place that sets out an action plan for improvement. This is usually educational opportunities that will enhance the employee's ability to do their job.

It is expensive to hire and train new employees. The goal is to retain good employees for the long term. By having a good solid pay for performance plan in place, the odds of motivating the employees and retaining them long term is excellent. I worked for the State of Oklahoma for years, and I was motivated to become a better employee by the educational opportunities they provided and the pay I received based on my performance.

Over the past several decades, many government agencies have switched to the pay for performance compensation to lessen the incentives to accept bribes in government atmospheres. It has been successful for the most part, but in countries such as Africa where corruption remains high, good employees get overlooked, and the crooked employees get big bonuses. It appears this might be an example for many third world countries. However, for the United States, pay for performance seems to be one of the top compensation plans (Sundström, 2019). I would anticipate it even becoming more in depth in the future.

Chapter 19 – Mental Health in the Workplace

Leaders are constantly challenged with mental health issues and employees. This is a complex area to manage and continues to be an important area of awareness. Anxiety and depression are rampant around the world for a lot of reasons. Stress and heavy workloads are the number one cause of mental health issues. Organizations, for the most part, do not measure the impact employees have on their workforce (Eager, 2017). One way to track mental health impacts in organizations is to create programs or initiatives that support healthy employees and a healthy workplace. In 2020, research discovered for every one dollar invested in wellness programs, organizations can expect to have two dollars and thirty cents return on their investment (Eager, 2017). Since that time, it has increased even more.

It is more important than ever, that organizations create special programs to address mental health issues. The past two years of COVID virus, loss of jobs, loss of homes, loss of money and resources along with relationships, have created enormous abnormal levels of stress. A lot of people died over the entire globe from this virus. People cannot be expected to be the same person after experiencing grief, illness, transition, hardships like the past two years. This is an area that is a hot spot and needs attention by every organization.

The latest on employee wellness programs measuring the ROI of Corporate Program Management can reach up to 300%, provided the right program is designed and well executed. Chronic disease management and preventive health promotion for employees and leaders can create long lasting positive results that impact everyone from the workplace to the home life, to the community they live in.

Chapter 20 – Ethical Exit Surveys

Many people who choose to leave an organization, are afraid to speak about the reasons why they are leaving. They fear this because of potential retribution, black balling, and bad recommendations for future employment elsewhere.

If an organization truly wants to be the best, they must be open to improvement, in all areas. Organizations can create what is called an ethical exit survey. On the last day of employment, the supervisor can provide the employee with a questionnaire and a stamped addressed envelope to drop into the mail once completed. Most likely, the employee will feel free to complete the survey honestly and mail it back.

Leadership of the organization can get together and create a list of questions for the ethical exit survey. Asking specific questions will help the organization to focus on what areas need to be addressed and changed. It is possible, a manager or supervisor has behaved unethically, or is a tyrant within his/her own department. Leadership needs to know these kinds of things.

This is one of the best things an organization can do if they truly want to be better in all areas.

Chapter 21 – Organizational Economics

Economics will continue to play an important role in all organizations, but I feel the healthcare industry will be most challenging. I believe an administrator needs to be creative when outlining goals and objectives for a facility. It is important to find ways to make a profit at the same time staying ahead of the competition. I feel if we reward people for being healthy it might motivate people to begin taking care of themselves and at the same time, cut down on unnecessary doctor and hospital visits. It will, in turn, benefit the organization.

As I look back over the past ten to twenty years, everything has increased in cost, yet wages have hardly improved over the years. This has made it difficult for families to do anything other than try to break even every month. When it comes to medical and the healthcare system, everything is sky high from services to the patients, to the medical supplies needed to take care of them. I believe it will always be about economics.

There must be a tool or a way to measure the cost of doing business and the benefits of doing business. A person needs to be able to allocate scarce resources in the best way possible. It takes a look at economics to do this (Dang, Likhar & Alok, 2016). Considering the economic realities of the health care field, better decisions can be made that will affect the pricing of services, reimbursements, and future investments of the facility.

The current healthcare system is a cluster, and it is important to look at all sides of the coin before making decisions. There are many healthcare facilities on top of their fields, while others struggle with everything. The patients have a lot to say about the type of care they receive and how much they think they should pay. However, you must balance that with the people who are in charge of the facilities budget and have authority on how much money needs to be spent to take care of patients. There are always economics involved when making decisions about the health care industry (Collyer, Willis & Lewis, 2017).

Chapter 22 – Importance of Analyzing Risks in Business

Businesses need to know if a decision is going to impact the company positively or negatively. Before a company decides, it is important to identify all the things that are negative that can impact long term and short-term decisions. When you list these negative risks and look at them deeply, you can then decide whether to move forward or not.

A bad decision can cost millions if not billions of dollars. To analyze those risks, you can transform data, uncontrollable variables, decision variables into output that will measure what will happen if these things are done. It is crucial that managers be able to predict the future output based upon data and unknown variables. "Management is a prediction of future results" (as quoted in Wood & Wood, 2005).

Risk is the possibility of an outcome that is not wanted. Analyzing risks can be done by using data that has been saved over the past or by using assumptions of the future. These variables can be changed to sharpen the outcome to one's desire. One important thing to remember is that programs and models need to be user friendly for those employees who are not familiar with programs such as Excel. The easier it is to use; the more likely employees will use it to measure known risks.

In the past, managers went with their gut feelings to estimate outcomes based on certain decisions that were made (Bonabeau, 2003). Today, it is important to know how to estimate how decisions impact the future.

Chapter 23 – Strategic Improvements for Business Meetings

Business meetings can be very stressful. Many organizations have so many meetings, it does not leave much time for employees to do their job. Everyone loves to be productive. Some organizations have meetings that are not needed, senseless, and time consuming. This alone, causes stress on everyone. While everyone is sitting at the non-important meeting, their minds are on other things, like how are they going to find the time to get their job done. There are many strategic considerations for meetings that can help organizations stay on track and stay focused.

In this day and time with the global business environment, it is important for everyone to be on the same page at the same time. When deciding whether to have a meeting it is important to determine first if it is necessary or not (Hynes & Veltsos, 2019). If the meeting is critical, then a manager would first need to determine what level of employee needs to be at the meeting. It could be supervisors at different levels or different department heads. It is also important to determine the topics that will be discussed, and these are best put on an agenda so the meeting can be kept to those topics (Hynes & Veltsos, 2019).

As a manager in the past, I have always made sure the who, when, where, why, and how is covered. It is important to know who needs to attend and who will be affected by the meeting (Hynes & Veltsos, 2019). It is important to set a date and time so all persons involved can attend or make arrangements to adjust their schedule or have someone attend for them. It is crucial to have a meeting place designated, otherwise everyone will be lost and not knowing where to be, at the given day and time. The manager setting up the meeting needs to understand why the meeting is important and how the information will be shared (Hynes & Veltsos, 2019). Sometimes, managers will need to share documents and distribute certain notices to other managers and employees. It is good to have all these documents ready and waiting at the meeting.

I have always set a time limit for my meetings. If during a meeting, someone wants to add last minute agenda topics, they have to table it to the next meeting so everyone can be prepared, and the last-minute topic doesn't get everyone off track.

A lot of meetings can be handled through emails. Some managers feel they have to have a meeting every week just because it is expected. However, most of the time, it is a waste of time. When a meeting happens, people groan and moan about being away from their job, just to attend another meeting. But, if meetings are kept strictly for very important topics, staff and managers will have more time to do their jobs and understand that when a meeting is called, it will be important.

It is important to have a person assigned to ensure minutes are taken of every meeting so there is a record of the meeting and the discussion and agreements on paper (Volkema & Niederman, 1996). In all meetings, the agenda, documents, and minutes are considered to be some of the most important items to not forget. It also is a nice touch when minutes of the meeting are distributed to people who were in attendance and to people who were absent. This can be handled via email, to conserve paper. You, as a leader, have the power to decide if the information can be shared via email or a meeting.

When leaders keep meetings reserved for important things, employees will begin to appreciate it. It sends a loud message to employees they are valued and so is their time. This is a very basic step towards holistic leadership.

Chapter 24 – Managerial Strategies for Interview Communications

When leaders interview applicants for a position, it is critical they take into consideration verbal and nonverbal answers, along with knowledge regarding different cultures. Selecting the right person for a job is very important. Remember, it is your job to build the best workforce the organization has ever had. Sometimes, it is necessary to hire specific persons to handle specific roles in the organization. If you have assessed the talent in your organization and do not have someone that can be developed into this future role, it is important to move forward and find the right person for the job. Globalization requires everyone to become aware of the diversified group of people available for jobs. This can mean many different things.

Leaders must include nonverbal answers as well as verbal answers when asking a question in the interview. Nonverbal cues are "everything but the words" (Hynes & Veltsos, 2019). Also, nonverbal cues can mean many things. What might mean one thing in the USA might mean the total opposite in another country. For example, wearing white as a bride in the USA is customary, in China it is saved for funerals or bereavement (Hynes & Veltsos, 2019). The nonverbal cues I believe to be vital in an interview are directness. If someone does not look you in the eye when you are talking to them, that is a sign of evasiveness and could mean they really do not qualify for the job. A person's dress or appearance is very important. If a person appears to an interview in flip flops, it demonstrates their feeling about the position. They are demonstrating they think the job is not important and more casual.

I have had this happen on several occasions. I had a receptionist position open in my X-ray company. I interviewed over fifty people for the vacancy. A receptionist is usually the very first impression of the organization. I needed someone with excellent communication skills and dressed appropriately. During this interview, two people arrived wearing Capri britches and flip flops. Both individuals acted as if they already had the job. This position sends a message to the customers and is the first impression of my company. If someone is wearing shorts or flip flops to work in a business environment, it will send a message to customers the company is lazy and does not care about how they appear to the community or customer. It will also send a message they have not done their research on the company. If they are applying for a job at a bank, then their dress should be conservative.

If a candidate sat with their arms crossed or legs crossed, this sends a message they are not open to talk about themselves or the job. If a person comes in and sits down and sits up straight leaning forward with a smile, they are ready for the interview. Also, someone that is polite and acknowledges everyone at the interview table will send a good message. A person that is open to communication will work well with others and not feel territorial.

There are signs that will alert you to the fact an applicant might be insincere and not right for the job. The way a person carries themselves will demonstrate their self-esteem and self -confidence. The clothing they wear will show how professional they will be in the office. Usually, a person dresses better for an interview than they do on the job because they want to make a good impression and get the job. If a person does not want to shake hands or look you in the eye, then they possibly have something to hide. This might mean they have lost a job before because of something they did, and they do not want you to know about it.

Also, if a person starts dropping names of high-ranking people in the community or corporation then they are relying on their friendship to get the job, not their personal accomplishments. Guilt and fear also enhance signs of stress in situations. This could be nervous twitching, speech hesitation and displays of fidgeting and restlessness (Porter, Doucette, Woodworth, Earle, & MacNeil, 2008).

A candidate's gender, ethnicity, and background could have a profound impact on how he or she communicates non-verbally. It is important to be aware of this. For example, if you ask a person from China how they would handle or decide on a particular example and they are hesitant in answering, it could be because in China, they do everything as a group. They do not have a word that means individualism. To them, selfishness is the closest thing. China is a collective culture, and they make decisions based on the "whole". Individualistic cultures like ours, has managers who want to make the decisions or at least talk to the person in charge (Hynes & Veltsos, 2019)

If a person interviewing for the job is from Sweden, Denmark, or Norway they are considered feminine countries and therefore value quality of life, children, and family more than money and things and assertiveness (Hynes & Veltsos, 2019). If the manager is looking for someone who is aggressive in sales and will do whatever it takes to complete a sale, a person from a feminine culture will answer differently than a masculine culture.

Recruiting and hiring can be a very stressful job. If you pick a person, you think is perfect only to discover later the person is the absolute worst employee ever, your staff will never let you forget it. They will expect you to do something about it, once you hire the person, but they will remind you, that person was your choice. Employees are funny about things like that.

It also works the other way around. I allowed two x-ray technicians to choose the person for the receptionist vacancy I had. I did this because they would be working directly with this person, day in and day out. However, the person they chose, was on the bottom of my pick list. But I gave them the benefit of the doubt, which made them feel valued.

This turned out to be short lived. The first day of the job, the girl was two hours late. The x-ray technicians had to answer the phones because their new girl did not show up on time. The second day, she was three hours late. Again, this put the x-ray technicians in a bind. The techs wanted her fired immediately. I reminded them, they chose her, and we need to make sure she had true emergencies. They assured me they did not want that responsibility again, in the future. By the third day, the new girl did show up on time, but was nowhere in sight and nobody was answering the telephones. I called over to see how things were going and nobody answered the telephone. I walked over to the x-ray company, and I found her in a back storage room, laying on the floor. I said to her, "You do realize you are the receptionist, and your job is to answer the phones?" When I asked her what she was doing, she responded, "I don't want to be a receptionist today". I responded, "Okay. I won't be needing you today. You can go home".

This example is great, because my x-ray techs based their decision to hire her solely on the way she dressed for the interview, which was sharp. My impression of the girl from the very beginning, was that she was evasive. She did not look me in the eye, not once, when I asked her questions about her experience and her qualifications. Her nonverbal cues led me to believe she was not only lazy, but possibly looking for a way to get unemployment for another six months.

She was fidgeting and very restless in her chair from the moment she arrived, until she left. In the end, she did file for unemployment and upon discussing the situation with the State of Oklahoma Unemployment claims officer, this person had a history of getting jobs and getting fired within a day or two. She never had intentions of being a receptionist. She did her best to get fired from the first day onward.

Selecting the interview panel is important. It is usually good to have a couple of employees or managers who work in the department the vacancy is for. However, as a leader, you can take into consideration the panel's top choices, but rely on your own personal experience to make a final decision. It really is difficult sometimes when you are trying to empower your employees and give them more authority than they usually have. In this case, it was the thought that counted. They appreciated it.

As our world connects to other countries, globalization has impacted the way we conduct interviews. In this day and time, many organizations rely on computer generated interviews because companies have expanded globally. The time it takes to travel and recruit for interviewing is very expensive. There are several things that can affect a job interview when it is done through a computer. First, a manager often relies heavily on first impressions of a person coming through the door to interview for a position. How a person carries themselves and whether they shake the interviewer's hand and look them in the eye is important (Hynes & Veltsos, pg. 411, 2019). When an interview is conducted through the internet, this is missing. Another important item is nonverbal body language. When a question is asked of a person during an interview, if the person shifts around in their seat and you can tell they do not want to answer that question, it will give the impression the person has something to hide. Also, if a person is embarrassed by a question or feels put on the spot, a manager is not going to see this because the person is not there personally to notice facial features or body language (Hynes & Veltsos, pg. 411, 2019).

The computer-generated interview might pick the best person for the job solely on qualifications and education. However, if the position is for a public service or customer service, it would be extremely important to see how the person handles themselves in person.

Managers interviewing potential employees via this medium must modify their interviewing strategy. I am a manager who likes to be in the middle of the hiring process from start to finish. I would be the one to sort the applicants to start with. Then, if it is necessary for a computer interview then I would want to follow up with some quality face time, perhaps a second interview. If it is not convenient to meet the person, then definitely doing face time through the internet or phone would be a necessity.

To make the best selection for the position, all things must be taken into consideration. There might be a person who has exceptional educational and work background but may not possess the necessary skills for the job. Another person might have the necessary exceptional skills but lack the educational background. If the interview is for a leadership position, it is equally important to have some type of person face to face contact with the person being interviewed.

Many companies utilize the internet to recruit people for face-to-face interviews. This is great when a manager does not have a lot of time to contact possible people to set up interviews. It also helps obtain a diverse group of potential applicants (Gundur, 2019). The important thing to remember is, a leader needs to get a good feel about the person's communication skills and people skills prior to making a decision. Communication is still the top skill needed for leadership. It is the top skill for management of any level. Therefore, you really need to see beyond a person's resume, to the whole person. A person is more than what you see.

Chapter 25 – Best Managerial Communication Tools

This chapter will discuss the managerial technological communication tools that are available to all managers in today's fast-paced business world.

There are five different tools used for communicating within networks of businesses (Hynes, & Veltsos, 2019). In the past five decades technology has advanced at such a pace it is hard to keep from overloading people, especially employees. However, electronic communication has been proven to be quite effective and efficient in sharing communication with employees. In many corporations, electronic communication is an essential part of every person's day.

Email is an excellent way to communicate, however, it also comes with potential sensory overload. A lot of managers can feel overwhelmed by an inbox of too many emails (Rosen, Simon, Gajendran, Johnson, Lee, & Lin, 2019). Many managers receive so many emails they need someone to sort them prior to opening them. Many corporations allow employees to work from home and employees stay connected through cell phones and tablets. These screens are small.

Therefore, it is critical, the email be well thought out and planned prior to being written so the email is short and to the point (Hynes, & Veltsos, 2019). If a message is urgent or extremely sensitive, the use of email is discouraged. There should be a face-to-face contact instead with the employees.

Emails are excellent for companywide notices. These can be created and submitted to include global employees around the world at a touch of the fingertip. If a message is to create conversations between employees, it is best to not use email as this is slow and confusing to follow. All employees should understand the company code of conduct regarding emails. Emails should only be used for business. Privacy issues should be addressed. Spam should be minimal and blocked. Many facilities have a department that oversees the information technology of all its employees. This is important as one department can create firewalls to block hackers and spam, to its user's computers. It is important to know what the time limit is for retaining messages and emails. Electronic messaging or instant texting is often used in the business world. It is acceptable when communicating with one or two people. The messages are in real time and can be transmitted instantaneously. However, sometimes, the person on the receiving end might be quicker in responding than the sender and the dialogue can become mixed. When a message is sent instantly, it saves time and can help when additional clarification might be needed. Text messages can also be legally binding, and if saved, can also protect a person from accusations of any kind. Text messages can also be binding in contractual agreements. If there is an offer, a consideration, and an acceptance it becomes legally binding (Hynes, & Veltsos, 2019).

Some of the disadvantages of texting include security issues. The message can be sent so fast it does not allow enough time for any type of software to check for viruses. Texting can also become very casual, and it is easy to slip into an unprofessional writing mode. This can be problematic if a person is trying to impress someone on the other end. It is important to not use instant messaging for highly sensitive or important confidential information. It is also recommended a policy be created within the agency to act as a guideline for employees. All messages can be saved through an archiving system on the cell phone. This ensures the messages can be retrieved later. When in a working capacity, it is prudent to always be professional whether instant messaging or emailing (Hynes, & Veltsos, 2019).

Blogging is a means of promoting and creating relationships with a variety of people. Blogging is basically websites that are updated daily or at least several times per week. Blogging can be used to advertise products and upcoming promotions. It is also a great tool to respond faster to complaints or issues that need to be resolved. It is important a Blog site be monitored closely as it is the voice of an organization. It is easy to receive a good reputation and as easy to receive a bad reputation. It is good to have a blogging policy and distribute it to all employees. Some organizations use blogs to recruit new employees (Hynes, & Veltsos, 2019).

Videoconferencing is a good way to connect teams around the world or even within a state. It is fairly inexpensive and can be connected through cell phones or tablets and computers. Documents can be shared along with open discussions and screen sharing. All that is required is an internet connection. This is an excellent way to conduct training to multiple places and people without having to pay for long distance travel and hotel expenses. Videoconferencing is great for building rapport between people and introducing new managers to the group. When hiring new people, it can be a good tool to use on a regular basis. This will help team members to feel closer to the corporate office and to other team members in remote areas (Hynes, & Veltsos, 2019). It is good to have a backup plan in case someone has a hard time connecting at a certain time. Many organizations rely heavily on audio or videoconferencing because the quality is good, and the communication is the same as if all parties were together (Habash, 1999).

Social networking is a big part of most organizations. Social networks such as Facebook is a good place to build an online presence for any organization. It is important the company has a policy regarding Facebook and all employees are made aware of the policy. Social networking is good for providing updates to the customers and employees. It is important to focus on building relationships with the customers and finding out what they want or need (Hynes, & Veltsos, 2019). It is also important to not share confidential information across the social network systems as it is immediately public.

It is important for any manager to think about which type of communication tool is right for the job and message they need to send. With technology becoming more advanced every day, managers are finding they have more responsibilities such as monitoring employee emails and text messages for professionalism, etc. (Hynes, & Veltsos, 2019).

In summary, there are many ways to communicate with employees in today's busy workforce. Technology is advancing at a fast pace and most organizations are utilizing emails, text messaging, videoconferencing, social media, and blogs to connect with customers and staff. Every means of communication tool has advantages and disadvantages. It is critical for the manager to decide what type of message needs to be sent, and to who, prior to choosing a method. It is important to archive all emails and text messages. This can be done on a cell phone or computer. This will also help in the overload of emails that might come in. Electronic communication has expanded and will continue to do so. It will be up to the managers to stay with the evolution of business communication and determine which type fits the business need the best.

Chapter 26 – IT for Managers

It is important to understand what creates value for an organization or company. Value drivers are what makes a product valuable and brings value to a customer, which in turn will create value for the company (Turban, Pollard & Wood, 2017). The three categories of value drivers are short term, medium term, and long term. The short-term drivers are operational, such as things that affect the cash flow of a company. An example could be what it might cost for material, mileage, sales volume, and sales revenue (Turban, Pollard & Wood, 2017). These types of drivers can change when the economy changes.

The medium value driver focuses on financial things such as debt of the company, working capital, bad debt expenses. Things that minimize the cost of capital incurred by the company that is needed to operate the business (Turban, Pollard & Wood, 2017).

Long term value drivers are what sustains the organization. These are the things that allow a business to thrive, prosper, and function for the long term. There are many things that can affect the long-term value drivers such as state and federal laws, regulations, privacy and security regulations and environmental laws (Turban, Pollard & Wood, 2017).

Many reactive approaches to IT investments fail. Many companies do not align their information technology needs to the business needs. This in turn, does not bring value to the company. Many companies want to have the top IT equipment. Sometimes this is not necessary, and it can be very costly and expensive to maintain, despite, maybe not being needed in the first place.

Leaders and managers need to be clear what the goal of IT business alignment is. The goal of IT business alignment is to achieve the company's strategic objectives. It is important to increase profitability and make the most out of its IT investment. The leaders of an organization must support the information technology department to have success. Otherwise, it can be miss-communicated and pieced together. The IT department needs to know and understand what the company's strategic plan and objectives the IT are, so can be part of that plan. It can affect the budget also. The IT department can give a company the competitive advantage and that is what every company wants (Turban, Pollard & Wood, 2017).

IT strategic planning should be revisited regularly because things change. The economy changes. The corporate environment can change and there might be threats from outside competitors that require immediate action that might not have been in the planning and strategic objectives. It is important to be flexible and knowledgeable about the entire IT system and objectives. It is advantageous for organizations to create a steering committee.

The steering committee will be a group of managers and supervisors from various departments. They will outline their goals and needs for the fiscal year. The group will prioritize these and establish a plan of action. In the plan of action, the direction will be set, and the corporate strategy becomes aligned with the IT strategy. This group will find the resources and approve all funds needed to meet the needs of the IT dept. All outsourcing decisions and policy are made by this group. The committee also shares information with the rest of the company along with establishing a type of performance measure to ensure the IT dept. is staying on target (Turban, Pollard & Wood, 2017). This group will create a strategic planning process.

The first step is to develop a strategic plan. The long-term plan is based upon the company's business plan. The IT dept. needs to know what it is going to take to achieve all the goals and objectives in the business plan. This long-term plan will encompass three to five years and will include such things as a budget, sourcing, resources, infrastructure, IT governance (Turban, Pollard & Wood, 2017).

The medium-term plan might consist of one to three years of more detailed information and steps to reach the long-term plan. It can break down the goals into realistic pieces and assign them to different personnel to focus on. This part of the phase will contain the project portfolio. This phase will have a list of management systems that are compatible with the long-term phase.

The third plan is to fine tune the budget and get more exact with the costs expected and planned for. This phase will also include a timetable that outlines the goals and time frames to be completed. This plan also can include things that are not expected, that might come up at the last moment and were not originally planned for.

All these phases should be evaluated and agreed upon by the group. A good IT strategy can help organizations gain a competitive advantage in the marketplace.

It can help companies take advantage of opportunities faster and more effectively. A company wants to create the best experience for the customer so they will return and not go somewhere else for the same product. A good IT strategy can be quick to update software or create an AP that might be useful for customers on their cell phones. It might help customers buy more if they can use their cell phone to complete a transaction.

A good strategic plan could increase profits for the company, be more innovative than usual, and even join business partners to create an even better vision for the company. Also, it could focus on security issues that might arise that normally would not. IT strategy is a complex thing looking from the engineering and design perspective because a company's strategy and governance can be different and complex (YoungKi & Mithas, 2020). When a company invests money into an IT enterprise system, it needs to provide value to that company (Gellveiler, 2017).

Chapter 27 – Best Communication Skills for Business

Women have a long history of building effective communication skills through social networks. These formal and informal networks lay solid foundations for women to be successful in a world of men. In today's global workforce it takes more than learning about finances, business analysis, and education to be successful. Women who empower others through positivity have a high success rate in business communication not only in their personal lives but their business lives as well. Women who create positive environments in business can apply their communication skills into strategic areas that will inspire, motivate, and in turn, change their company into a more dynamic organization. The best communication concepts for women in business include the power of positivity, creating informal and formal networks, being empathetic and patient, goal oriented and assertive. When women work to empower other women through networking and business communications, no matter how small or large their network is, they are playing a huge role in the global movement of positive change.

Women have been creating informal networks of all kinds for thousands of years. Women tend to be more empathetic and share strong positivity with all those they encounter. These networks of people have helped inspire many women to follow their dreams of becoming business owners and executives in the corporate world. Networking is a smart way to create, build, and strengthen relationships through sharing information (Hynes & Veltsos, 2019). Women who are focused on their goals and are persistent, are headed for success. To be successful in networking, a person should be open minded, empathetic, prepared, and educated in diversity in the workplace. Women are empowering each other to become transformational leaders in the business world today.

During the early seventeen and eighteen hundreds, women transformed the way the world viewed them. For hundreds of years, women were the ones who stayed home and took care of the family. As the New World was evolving, women from Europe, especially the Dutch and the French seized the great opportunities to create networks of all kinds. These networks allowed women to communicate and build businesses that offered products that others never had or even heard of (Todt, 2015). Governments including the American, Dutch, and French kept records of how successful women were in the business communities. Business owners kept records of all the activities that were generated between women and their informal networks. It was not long, women were no longer just workers in a business, but a legitimate business owner (Todt, pg. 153, 2015). The Dutch women aggressively sought and created networks with the Native Americans and developed the Fur trade. These same women seized the great opportunities to sell their handmade clothing and supplies to the French Colonial military regime. This created freedom and great wealth for women in the early days. They counted on these informal networks to share information and encourage other women to become self- employed.

Networking can be a very powerful management tool for business communication for men and women (Hynes & Veltsos, pg. 435, 2019). It takes time to build strong relationships in business. Sharing information, however, is a good way to strengthen business relationships (Hynes & Veltsos, pg. 435, 2019). Networking is strengthened when one person can share potential customers and both parties have a solid trust with each other. Everyone involved can save time, save money, earn money, when one party refers business clientele or employees with another. When this is done, a reputation of generosity is what makes the network contact worth keeping (Hynes & Veltsos, pg. 435, 2019). Many companies ignore the vast opportunities that await them with informal networking, and they only respect the more formal networks within their organizations. However, even today, more and more leaders are relying on these informal networks to build their careers and to strengthen their business communication skills. When companies talk about inspiring, motivating, and transforming employees and their organizations, these things rely on communication (Todt, pg. 261, 2015).

Many organizations today want more from their leaders. When interviewing a potential leader or manager, they are looking for people who love life, who are excited and full of energy. Many top leaders around the globe are full of passion (Meek, Tucker, Pueschel, & Jordan, pg. 1, 2019). A person's professional outlook is equally important as their academic or experience capabilities. It is important to look at the whole person, along with their life experiences.

People who are happier and more positive with themselves are more likely to be promoted as managers and agency leaders (Meek, Tucker, Pueschel & Jordan, pg. 3, 2019). Managers and leaders who have more self-esteem and well-being, are more authentic and real. When these employees rely on their own beliefs, values, and strengths, they become leaders who help others to change. This type of leadership will create a very positive environment and performance by employees with high morale and longevity.

Organizations who create a positive environment reinforces the resilience of problem solving within an agency. This environment will embrace empathy and respect for each other, from employees to customers (Meek, Tucker, Pueschel & Jordan, pg. 3, 2019). Goal setting and having classes on vision boards create positive environments in business.

Research is being conducted to add Positivity as a crucial concept in business communication (Meek, Tucker, Pueschel & Jordan, pg. 8, 2019). Corporations can also add lectures or additional educational classes for their employees to help foster this environment. Many ways to create a positive impression include asking how a person is doing and getting to know the employee. Also, asking what that person is thankful for that day is also a way to bring out positive emotions and good feelings. Building positive networks within an organization and outside an organization will strengthen a leader's relationship and ultimately all human resource capital.

Women of all countries are constantly creating informal networks. Many women who have immigrated to other countries are creating businesses and building successful careers and lives, while staying connected to their home countries (Webster, 2017). Globalization has increased the opportunities for women to build informal networks in rural and remote locations. These women are very active, daily in their routines, using this means of communication to strengthen all the networks they create. Women are responsible for a big role in developing remote areas and even more in whole regions. Women are often connected though social interaction and can sell their products, whether it is something they made or agriculture items. Many of these women take advantage of creating informal networks to promote themselves in the business world. In remote and rural areas, networking is very powerful because the connections are so deeply rooted in the day-to-day activities (Webster, 2017). Many businesswomen use these networks to create solid income, so they can support their families in their home country.

In the past, women had a harder time successfully communicating in the corporate world because it was considered a man's world. Over the years, women have moved past this barrier and learned how to become more assertive and goal oriented. It is important for women as exceptional leaders and managers to develop excellent communication and problem-solving skills. To identify a problem, take the time to think things through with a plan to solve the problem, and communicate the problem to higher ups, takes skill (Berry, 2010). Developing excellent communication skills takes time and practice. A successful manager will deal with a problem right away. Some managers ignore problems until they fester and then they become bigger problems, even they cannot solve. These types of managers will never promote higher than they are because they are afraid of problem solving, and the communication skills that are needed, to get the job done. Some people respond too quickly, but this can be considered impulsive. Some leaders think they are responding quickly, when in fact, they are reacting to a situation. It is best to think the problem through and create a positive solution (Berry, 2010).

For managers to become excellent communicators in leading a team, a manager needs to learn how to delegate (Berry, 2010). Many women in leadership and management positions try to do it all and end up exhausted. However, it is so important for managers to involve their team as this will foster good morale and motivation (Berry, 2010). A lot of women feel they have something to prove, and so when they try to do it all themselves, they feel they are responsible for it all. Real strength in communication comes from creating more productivity. All team members should be assigned a specific role with a deadline and responsibilities. The manager must make very clear expectations of all team members. When a woman leader learns how to effectively communicate to her team, she will save herself a lot of heartache, time, and in turn, create championship teams. This will cinch her reputation and will go a long way in promoting her throughout the agency (Berry, 2010). This will foster a very positive environment for her department and agency.

Many women have a difficult time communicating with men, in corporate leadership. Sometimes, it is because the woman feels at a disadvantage from the beginning. When, in fact, we all put our pants on, one leg at a time. No person is better than the other. It takes all leaders, working together, to create excellence of an unimaginable magnitude. Some women feel they must work harder and become overachievers, to pass by the big egos of some co-workers. The glass ceiling is very real in some organizations, still. Not all organizations embrace female leaders. This is so unfortunate. Leadership can only become excellence, themselves, when they embrace diversity.

In these organizations where women struggle to become part of the leadership team, reality is a very different world. In these circumstances, when women have problems at home, it is best to leave those problems at home. It is important to maintain a positive and professional attitude, and communication style, always. If you are fortunate to work in an environment that embraces diversity, and the whole person, then things are a lot different and better. Although women have come a long way, there is still a lot of work to do. Always, women should embrace their strengths, value themselves, and keep building upon their skills to become a holistic leader. Women should become goal oriented, focused, and become mentors and role models for others. Most of all, women should follow the dreams that are held dear, and keep building their networks.

The culture of an organization is reflected by the culture between managers and the staff. If a negative culture exists within an organization, it is critical to change the negative environment to a positive environment to ensure the best possible outcome in performance (Miftari, pg. 263, 2015). The culture is based upon the leaders and managers own personal style of communication. If the relationships within an organization are strengthened with more positivity, the company will respond outwardly with a more positive business culture (Miftari, pg. 263, 2015).

It is more important to create positive change than to just communicate when it comes to global leadership (Miftari, pg. 260, 2018). A manager must be able to convey his/her belief in the message that is being said to the other party. It is extremely important for a company to be received as credible and of authority to the audience to make the right ethical decisions (Miftari, pg. 260, 2018). Building networks within an organization will help support managers. When a manager can inspire and motivate employees to move toward his/her vision and goals, and truly believing it is for the best interest of the employees, the company, and the community, he/she then becomes a transformational leader (Miftari, pg. 261, 2918).

Over the past fifty years it has been determined that by empowering women all over the world to improve their lives, it has become one of the most important parts of international development (Coleman, 2010). Although there are still those countries where women are inferior and suppressed, with the global movement in business, even those countries are seeing that if they want to be part of the new global marketplace and business, they must invest in the empowerment of women. Women are assets to any leadership team.

Business skills and communication skills and other educational opportunities are being offered around the world. The World Bank is partnering with private entities that have spent years promoting the empowerment of women. By empowering women and investing in women around the world, it will reduce poverty and hunger all the while promoting growth in remote and rural parts of the world (Coleman, 2010). The informal and formal networks that are already in place in these remote and rural parts of the world will have a jump-start in this movement.

Networking possibilities are endless. Anyone can begin building informal or formal networks at any time. Some resources of potential networks could be through family, friends, past co-workers, schools, employers, or even neighbors. A person can volunteer in areas of need or of interest in the community. Becoming a new member in a social network in the community is often very productive because most members are also professionals and know the community. Social media offers Facebook and LinkedIn to meet other people of all kinds and from around the globe. Being a good listener and promoting skills and strengths, will help find good networking opportunities. First impressions are always important, so it is critical to be dressed professionally and keep in mind the way a person acts will be what is remembered. Above all, learn how to create a positive image that can earn an excellent reputation. It takes time to develop skills and attributes that are necessary in communicating with others. When a manager builds networks, formal or informal, that manager is practicing every day to be a better person. Networking is a very resourceful way to build a business and to empower others at the same time.

Chapter 28 – Leadership Writing Skills and How it Can Affect Morale

The success of a manager and the company is dependent upon the quality of communication shared. Managers spend most of their time communicating between customers, employees, and upper managers. Managerial writing skills are critical because the way a person shares a message can be received as positive or negative (Hynes & Veltsos, (2019). The message is also a permanent record, so the quality is very important.

All records can be scrutinized in a court of law (Hynes & Veltsos, 2019). This alone, is reason to display excellent writing skills. What a manager puts on paper can be supportive of his company or otherwise. It is always important to understand all documents can be public.

When a manager writes an email or other form of message, it is crucial to think about the message being sent. How a manager words a message can determine how a person on the other end receives it. A manager needs to make sure all the basics are covered in the message such as what, why, when, how, and who (Hynes & Veltsos, 2019). The planning stage is critical prior to writing the message. The words used can strengthen morale, the culture, the motivation, and the collaboration of all persons in the agency or it can tear it down.

A manager should give very careful thought as to the words that will be used. A manager wants to make sure the message comes across the way it is intended. A message should be short and to the point. It is better to use short words than long drawn-out phrases that might seem out of place or confusing to the receiver. It is better to use more specific words than to use general words. Specific words and phrases will catch the reader's attention (Hynes & Veltsos, 2019).

In addition, it is better to keep whole sentences short. When a person spends too much time trying to understand what a sentence means, it is too long. Good sentences should be no longer than fifteen to twenty words. Mangers do not want to confuse the reader or reduce the importance of a message by making it too long (Hynes & Veltsos, 2019).

The ability to write well is crucial to advancement in an organization. Excellent writing skills are valued very highly by upper management (Bennett & Rhodes, 1988). A lot of managers will look for positions that are equal to their writing skills. Some employees are apprehensive about jobs that require skillful writing. Many managers deal with intensive writing due to strict deadlines or knowing the writing will be scrutinized by higher ups (Bennett & Rhodes, 1988). Local junior colleges offer many writing classes and employees and managers alike can always improve their business writing skills through personal development.

Managers are responsible for communicating with customers, employees, shareholders, and many other people. Writing memos or emails or letters do not necessarily mean they need an answer, however, many letters or emails received do require some type of response. The skill of writing is considered a necessity for managers (Hynes & Veltsons, pg. 219, 2019). There are two strategies of inquiries, direct and indirect.

Direct inquiry is used for sharing information that contains good news or neutral information (Hynes & Veltsons, pg. 222, 2019). Some managers lose the interest of the receiving party because they put the good news or message somewhere in the middle or end of the letter. The letter should start off with the main point. Starting a letter off with a big point or main theme that answers the person's question will help strengthen the positive impact of the response (Hynes & Veltsons, pg. 222,

2019). The body of the letter should always support the opening statement. This might include instructions or policy or requirements in the positive response. A direct inquiry always should close on a positive ending. A simple thank you can do wonders.

Indirect inquiry is used when the message being sent is not what the receiving party might be wanting to hear. Every manager will sometime have to write a letter declining a request or terminating someone. In this type of inquiry, the main point should be later in the letter. A manager should build up to the main point as to soften the blow, sort of speak (Hynes & Veltsons, pg.223, 2019). A good start is to let the person down softly. For example, in a termination letter, the manager could begin with pointing out the person's strength and character and skills. Then, slowly go into the reasons why a layoff is happening or a termination. The goal is to build relationships, not tear them apart. The closing of an indirect inquiry should always end in goodwill (Hynes & Veltsons, pg. 223, 2019). Wishing a person good luck or well wishes will stay with that person.

The Pollyanna hypothesis is that positive words are used more than negative words in writing (Hildebrandt & Snyder, 1981).

Positive words are by far more meaningful than negative words. When writing any letter, whether good or bad news, a manager should always remain positive in their words. In 1969 when the Pollyanna hypothesis came about, the intentions were never intended for business communications. However, over the past forty years or so, it has been adapted by the business community and recommended as a style of writing for managers.

Chapter 29 – Organizational Annual Reports

Annual reports are one of the most important documents a corporation can write. Annual Reports help companies to stay on track with their organizational goals and missions. They provide data and critical information to key stakeholders and potential investors. Banks can look at annual reports to evaluate whether a credit needs to be adjusted or evaluated. Annual Reports will clearly and concisely show an organization's performance for the past twelve months. These reports can also be compared to prior years to calculate the progress of a company.

Annual Reports are important to key stakeholders because they will include a summary as to the true status of finances, goals, objectives, and executive summary. The Annual Report is a formal report with a title page, transmittal document, table of contents, list of illustrations, and executive summary (Hynes & Veltos, 2019). The report itself will have introductions, major headings that separate the areas, closing summary along with recommendations. If needed, a report can list references or appendix (Hynes & Veltos, 2019). Annual Reports should be written in a concise and clear manner. The format should be easy for anyone to understand and read. The Annual Report helps build trust in the community and with stakeholders alike. It demonstrates integrity and trustfulness.

Chapter 30 – Nonverbal Behavior

This chapter will discuss the key issues and underlying issues related to nonverbal behavior. Managers rely daily on their ability to communicate with all persons they come into contact. This might be customers who have complaints and wish to speak to a manager. This also includes direct communication with all employees. Many managers develop skills over time that help them understand what a person is really saying to them. Communicating is a very complex process that includes more than words. Nonverbal communication will include a person's expression, body posture, and their appearance (Hynes & Veltsos, pg. 306, 2019). It is up to both parties to pay attention and decipher the actual message that is being transmitted between persons.

Signals received from a person through nonverbal communication almost always have more than one meaning. The signal adds depth to the words a person is saying. These signals can be influenced by the environment a person comes from. Nonverbal communication is different depending on the country, region, or social class a person has come from. Nonverbal signals can also demonstrate whether a person is telling the truth or not. Some people demonstrate nonverbal signals that do not support the spoken words they are saying. In these circumstances, a manager can consider the nonverbal signals and can trust the person is saying one thing but meaning another (Hynes & Veltsos, pg. 306, 2019).

Nonverbal communication has many functions: complementing, accenting, contradicting, repeating, regulating, and substituting (Hynes & Veltsos, pg. 326, 2019). Nonverbal communication complements the words and adds weight to what is being said. The sender wants their message heard and when a person uses nonverbal signals to enhance what they are saying, it will be received loud and clear.

Nonverbal communication also includes the way a person moves. It could include a way a person holds their head while they are speaking. It could be the way a person is standing or walking. It could mean a person has prolonged eye contact than normal. Movement also includes the way a person uses their hands to gesture as they speak. There are four different spatial zones around a person that says a lot about a person who is trying to communicate with another (Hynes & Veltsos, pg.313, 2019). All persons are keenly aware of their own intimate spatial zone. This is a certain space that is closest to a person. When someone steps into a person's intimate space, many people get uncomfortable, especially when the relationship is not of an intimate kind. There are also personal, social, and public spatial zones around a person. When a person is communicating with another and they step pass the acceptable zone, a person can get an entirely different message than what is being said.

A manager's appearance is very important also when communicating with employees. It is important for a manager to be aware of their grooming habits that include clothing, makeup, hairstyle. A manager's appearance should support the customer and company expectations. How a manager speaks will also send nonverbal communication clues. The tone of the voice along with the pitch and duration of the conversation can speak volumes (Hynes & Veltsos, pg. 326, 2019). Although it is important for managers to establish professional relationships with their staff, there is a line that should not be crossed. If a manager crosses the line and their nonverbal communication makes a staff member uncomfortable, then the manager has created an unprofessional situation that will be addressed sooner or later.

It usually takes time for a manager and employee to develop a trusting professional relationship. Once this happens, the manager and employee will usually stay within the personal spatial zone of communication. It is important for managers to respect the spatial zones between supervisor and employee. Once a manager steps from personal space into an employee's intimate space, problems will arise that will need to be addressed. "Research on nonverbal behavior indicates that standing close to others may be interpreted as dominance" (Pavlich, Rains & Segrin, 2017). The employee could feel threatened because the supervisor is his/her boss and if he/she does not comply, he/she might lose their job. This could lead to losing a very valuable employee or a manger themselves could lose their job. A manager should always maintain a professional spatial zone between employees and keep the relationship on a business level. Effective communication is the cornerstone of success in the business world (Oliver, 2019). Managers must be aware of the messages they are sending to every person they communicate with. Trust is a foundation of business communication. It is important for managers to develop a trusting relationship with subordinates to successfully manage productivity and organizational goals and missions. It is equally critical a manger never abuses that trust by crossing the line with nonverbal communication that makes a subordinate feel uncomfortable.

Chapter 31 – Fostering a Listening Climate

Leaders are responsible for fostering a listening climate within their organization. Changing the listening climate can indeed reverse low morale.

A manager can create a positive climate in the workplace by trying to understand and connecting with the person's feelings. If an environment does not have a safe environment where people feel they can speak freely, the climate will have a low morale. A good manager can foster a very positive environment by being open and attentive when an employee is talking to them and possibly even jotting down some notes (Hynes & Veltsos, pg. 290, 2019).

A manager wants to have a good trusting working relationship with everyone in the company and office. This does take time because a lot of people just say what they think the upper management wants to hear. They do not feel as if they matter or what they say will be heard. It takes time and many interactions between employees and their managers to develop this trust to the point the environment will reflect it. The micro listening climate can change to the negative if a manager's non-verbal communication is saying the opposite of his verbal communication (Hynes & Veltsos, pg. 290, 2019).

A macro listening climate is when a manager walks around and always makes him or herself available. If an environment was one of authoritative prior, it can be changed if a new manager makes the effort. Actively being involved and being seen around in the various departments, using the same break room and rest rooms can also send a positive message of availability. If a manager likes to communicate one on one instead of relying on emails, it also sends a positive message the manager wants to have contact with the employees. In addition, if a manager takes the time to get to know every person, this will build a strong relationship over time. This is not about micro-managing your people. This is about being available and open to developing long lasting professional relationships, and creating the best workforce the organization has ever had.

A manager that does not have good listening skills will eventually lead to problems in the business (Rame, 2011). It is important to develop active listening skills to improve productivity in the workplace. Many managers have bad habits when it comes to listening skills. This might include, for example, to keep on working on something even though someone comes into the office to speak to you. It only takes a second to put down the pen or stop typing on the computer and be present and actively listen to the employee. This is a classic example of the great opportunity to demonstrate employee value. People feel valued when they know what they are saying is not falling on deaf ears. A manager can practice being a good listener by paraphrasing and asking questions. A manager also needs to be approachable (Hynes & Veltsos, pg. 298, 2019).

Chapter 32 – Cultural Communications

I will discuss the reasons why it is important for managers of all kinds and levels to understand and learn about diversity in the workplace, and the ways managers adapt to global diversity.

With the digital age and electronics, countries have been able to network and reach out around the world. Corporations and facilities are expanding their horizons by looking for ways to reduce their expenses and cost of manufacturing products and at the same time, increase their annual sales. As more and more countries expand into other regions of the world, it has become a necessity for employees to learn new languages and cultures. Failure to do so can result in disastrous business communications and business deals around the world. Communicating globally is more than just learning about diversity. It is about expanding the corporate vision and perspectives to a world-wide view to not only include diverse business practices or new ways of thinking, but to include actual diverse skills and talent (Hynes & Veltsos, 2019).

The new leaders of tomorrow must learn how to communicate effectively and create successful leadership in other parts of the world. Every country has its own diverse work ethics and ways of doing things. It is up to the organizations going to those countries to discover and train their own employees about the ethics and protocols that are acceptable in that country. The Human Resource Management department is responsible for educating employees about global and domestic cross-cultural differences (Hynes & Veltsos, 2019). Human Resource departments in organizations are the ones who make major decisions regarding people management.

Language plays a huge role in managing diversity across the world. The human resource management departments must find ways to share the same information in many languages. For example, a company that has employee manuals full of policy and procedures and ethical guidelines must be translated into the appropriate languages so employees in other countries understand the company and its missions and goals (Selected Cross-Cultural Factors in Human Resource Management, 2008). The success of a company depends upon all employees knowing the rules. Understanding language includes learning to read body language as well. For example, in India, the usual nodding yes of a head, means no. This can create problems and confusion on the receiving end and will need to be addressed by learning the behavior of that country and adapting. In addition, not everyone speaks fluent English. A great leader will never assume English is the first language.

When a manager is working with a diverse culture, it is important to remember to speak correct English and keep the slang terms or phrases out of the business room. This will enable the manager to get the message across more clearly without confusion. A good manager will be empathetic and non-judgmental while addressing cultural diversity (Hynes & Veltsos, 2019). It would be prudent for any manager, if they knew they were going to be on a global assignment, to get as much knowledge as they can, to prepare them for the transition. It is especially important to learn about expected greeting rituals and how to respectfully communicate with others. It is also equally important to learn the appropriate dress requirements.

Fairness in the workplace is important among all cultures. Although, it might be more important for Americans to be treated fairly when it comes to wages, services, and other important areas of business. Americans are more likely to leave a position if they feel they are being treated unfairly.

It is crucial for managers to create a workplace that builds relationships based upon respect and encourages employees to share their ideas and skills. Many managers and employees look for work elsewhere when they feel they are not respected. Human Resource Management departments can provide educational training on sensitivity and accepted behavior in the workplace (Selected Cross-Cultural Factors in Human Resource Management, 2008).

Cultural decision making is different in many countries. It is important to understand who makes the decisions, why and how decisions are made prior to jumping in and making decisions the way managers are used to. It is important to realize and appreciate the hierarchy of a country. For example, in the USA, it is normal for managers to obtain input from lower-level employees. This gives the employees a feeling they matter to the organization. In some countries, only the owners or very high level, make the decisions. They make the decisions without any input from lower-level employees. Human Resource Management departments can create many different types of change management training to help assist the managers with cultural decision making.

Many agencies rely on quarterly or yearly employee performance evaluations. In the USA many promotions are based on whether an employee has been productive, efficient, and has knowledge and skills. In many other countries where employees are taught from birth, to work for the higher good and, employee evaluations for one person might be considered harsh. It is important to understand this and provide feedback in a subtle manner that is not aggressive or confrontational to the employee. Miscommunication can happen very easily, especially in countries that rely on facial expressions and tone in addition to words.

Organizational learning is critical in a global business environment. Prior to sending a new manager to another country it is important the new manager be educated on how to provide feedback to employees of another country. The Human Resource dept. can also place the new manager with a mentor for a time period to share real life experiences and knowledge of the country he/she is expected to travel to (Selected Cross-Cultural Factors in Human Resource Management, 2008).

Instilling a global mindset in all managers will create a strong and diverse workforce. A manager that is successful in managing across all boundaries including organizational and functional in other countries will be a strong asset within an organization. Organizations can create advanced training within to speed up the process of educational learning for managers. Creating a global mindset is good for domestic and global markets. Customer service is required in every culture and the domestic business market is as diverse as the global business market.

Human Resource Management departments are key stakeholders in the success or failure of adapting to global diversity. It is extremely important for managers to learn the values of countries where business will be conducted. Developing educational and in-house training programs will educate all employees and prepare staff to have a global mindset. Managers in the human resource departments are responsible for managing people in the organization. This includes financial decisions along with hiring and termination practices (Selected Cross-Cultural Factors in Human Resource Management, 2008).

The human resource department can create a cultural global mindset within the agency by reviewing the way things are done in the present. This could include appropriate language and body behavior. Successful cross-cultural communication occurs when a person can learn verbal, non-verbal and values of a country (Davidovitch, & Khyhniak, 2018). A major asset for all managers is to have empathy for the people they are working with. It is important to be open and willing to learn new ways and understanding why the culture does things differently (Jiang & Wang 2018).

Managers who have experienced problems in the global market can share their experiences with human resource management and assist in finding ways to change wherever change is needed. Cross cultural empathy is a key to strengthening cross cultural communication (Jiang & Wang 2018). Mentoring programs along with in-house value-based culture training can be developed and added to on-boarding programs. Human resource management can adapt training programs to be tailor made for specific countries. It is critical human resource management take the lead on cultural diversity.

Every country is different and experiencing political and economic issues. It is important to be up to date on these serious issues in case a national crisis occurs while in another country. Awareness of all key topics can be lifesaving. If a country is not considered safe, an emergency exit strategy must be in place, prior to sending someone to that country.

Chapter 33 – Conflict Resolution Skills for Leaders

There are many skills I feel are important to all managers, at every level. The most fundamental skills include conflict resolution, excellent communication skills, and cultural diversity communication skills.

I feel all managers should be trained and skilled in intervention methods and conflict resolution. Every organization has conflict of some sort. Not all conflict is negative because it is important to have different views and perceptions to come to a middle ground and understand the entire picture. This is the first time in history where five generations of people are working together in companies. When you think about this, it is important that managers understand every generation has a different upbringing and perception of situations (Hynes & Veltsos, 2019).

It is important for managers to have the skills of creating dialogue between workers. If a manager forms a strong opinion about a conflict, this will interfere in conflict resolution. The manager needs to be open minded and create a safe place for all workers to express their viewpoints and opinions so that a resolution can be reached (Hynes & Veltsos, 2019).

It is important to become skilled in cultural diversity. When a manager can manage diverse viewpoints, more positive and creative outcomes are possible (Hynes & Veltsos, 2019).

These skills are extremely important because excellent communication skills will help managers to share values and individual perceptions which can often lead to conflict. If these skills are developed, once the shared values and individual perceptions are out in the open, people tend to relate or understand what the other side is considering to be important.

Many people take things to heart and feel as if it's between "me and you" when it comes to conflict resolution. However, as a manager, creating a feeling of its about "us" will create a safe environment and conflict can be resolved easily (Shapiro & Shackleton, 2019). In addition, if one person or group feels less important or perceived to be less than the other group, this will add to the conflict and it will be more difficult to resolve (Thomson, Overall, Cameron & Low, 2018). It is important for managers to be able to feel the dynamics that are going on in any type of conflict. To get a good feel for a situation, a manager must have excellent instincts and good communication skills.

There are many conflict resolution strategies that can be utilized. It is important to evaluate the situation and find your own personal approach that works best.

I have always tried to solve problems with a problem-solving approach. Years ago, in the early 1980's, The State of Oklahoma Department of Corrections sent me for certification in Mediation training. This was the most beneficial training I have ever attended. This problem-solving approach is what I learned. When I mediated between offenders and victims, it seemed easy to reach a consensus of resolution. It was more difficult for me to remain impartial when a victim was a child that had been molested.

Over the years, I have tried to use this same approach in my businesses and with my employees. However, there have been a time or two in the past forty years, that my emotions were high, and I was not open to a discussion of anything. This, of course, led to loss on both sides. Again, a good lesson learned.

In the problem-solving approach there are four beliefs that a manager must have. The first belief is that cooperation is better than competition. The manager must be willing to be open and have good listening skills. To build a strong team, everyone must cooperate.

The second belief is that managers must go into the situation believing everyone can be trusted. If one manager is not trustful of someone, it will immediately be felt by the other parties. In turn, they will not trust the manager. Only trust someone until they give you reason not to trust them any longer (Hynes & Veltsos, 2019).

The third belief is that managers believe the rank of someone, or status power can be minimized while trying to resolve a conflict. If not, then the lower employees will feel they really do not have a say in the resolution. They may bend to the will of a superior (Hynes & Veltsos, 2019).

The fourth belief is that there are solutions that can be found that are mutually acceptable for all parties involved (Hynes & Veltsos, 2019). If one party believes there is not a solution happy for all, then one party will lose. Both parties need to believe there are solutions that can make everyone happy.

These four beliefs along with excellent appropriate communication skills and paraphrasing will help settle any type of conflict a manager has.

I have learned a lot, using this type of conflict resolution approach. It makes me stop and think before I open my mouth to speak. To me, it is more important to respond instead of reacting to conflict. Sometimes, I need to walk away for a bit and think about the issue and then respond when I have thought it all through. I do not take things personal any longer, like I did when I was in my twenties. Keeping an eye on the bigger picture has helped me a lot, in communication with my employees. There are times, also, when it is better to remain silent. Some situations require you to absorb everything that is going on at the time and then retreat to put everything into perspective. If you respond before you have thought out what you need to say, then everything you say can be misconstrued if not put in the proper context.

Chapter 34 – Don't Be a Groupthink

Groupthink is a tendency to go along with the consensus of the group even if you do not agree with what they decided. Many organizations make decisions that affect lives of not only customers, but employees. It is important to not rush into decisions, especially when lives are at stake. It is important for all persons involved to be actively involved in the decision making and voicing opinions and what if questions. All persons on a team, play an essential role, and it is important to not follow, just for the sake of following.

There have been many instances in history when information has surfaced at the last minute that demanded safety changes to products, but due to the pressure of leadership or even the public, decisions were made to continue. People have died. Many organizations employ top level engineers for a reason. When an engineer brings up topics of concern to leadership, they should listen. Engineers should work together to form a strong opposition of launching a product, until safety issues are corrected.

It is important to ask every person involved their opinion and why they feel the way they do. I think many people have a hard time doing anything but groupthink, because of all the pressure from leadership. It is important for someone in the group to play the devil's advocate and ask, what if this happens, what are we going to do? All these types of decisions should be based on doing the right thing for the right reasons. Many people have died over the years because employees are afraid to speak their minds.

Group think can happen in any organization or business. Sometimes when a team member is silent then that is considered their consent. However, some persons might feel pressured to not speak up and voice their concerns because they might receive backlash or lose their job even. Many team members will go along because they want to get along with their group, and this makes it ripe for groupthink to even happen (Valine, 2018).

As managers, we have an obligation and duty to voice our opinions and offer counter arguments. We are paid to do just that and to find the best solutions and outcomes for whatever project we are working on. As managers we need to spend more time on deductive reasoning, honesty, and integrity so we can be proud of who we are and what we accomplish.

Chapter 35 – Management Communication Systems

There are several types of management communication systems. In this chapter, I will talk about the scientific management and the administrative management theory.

The scientific management system is truly a one-way communication between managers and employees. The employee is expected to abide by the rules and policy that the company has created without question. There is never any room for negotiation or discussion with the scientific management system (Hynes, & Veltsos, 2019).

The administrative management system came into play around the same time as the scientific management system. The difference is the administrative system focused on discipline and maintaining some type of order without the need for discussion or good listening skills. Employees were expected to obey without questioning any of the superior managers. There was usually a chain of command from the top-level managers to the lowest level of managers and the chain of command must always be adhered to (Hynes, & Veltsos, 2019). The issues with this type of management style, was the time it took to get approval or authority from top level managers to the lower level of managers, making the system inefficient and ineffective. Henri Fayol was responsible for the administrative management system theory which discipline played a large part. The ways of communicating have changed over the past thirty-five years due to the evolution of the technological age (Soares, 2018). Thank goodness for technology.

In the early nineteen eighties, I worked for a company that built automotive starters and alternators. When the company opened for business, they had spent a lot of money on promoting the company and they hired fifteen hundred employees to begin manufacturing, at the Oklahoma plant. I was one of the first fifteen hundred people hired. On the very first day of my job, I was assigned a post. My supervisor was a woman. She told me my job was to take a flat piece of sheet metal from the fifty-five-gallon drum on my left and place the piece of sheet metal on the huge drill press in front of me. The drill press was about seven feet tall, and it was automated with a two-inch drill bit that came down every fifteen seconds.

My job was to drill a two-inch hole in each flat piece of sheet metal, remove it from the drill press and place it into another fifty-five-gallon drum on my right. When the fifty-five-gallon drum on my left was empty, it was my job to get a commercial dolly, and load the full drum onto it. I was told to take it to the acid room. Once I had reached the acid room, I then grabbed hooks from a huge chain and placed the hooks on either side of the barrel. Once I had the barrel secured, I used a wench to lift it up, over, and down into a large vat of acid to clean. Once that process was complete, I was to return to my post and begin drilling from a new drum of sheet metal.

The supervisor told me I could not take a break or lunch until I had completed at least three fifty-five-gallon drums of metal. My quota for a day's work was six drums of metal parts. The first day, I had to stand in one spot the entire day, without a break or lunch, because I did not even get through one drum. The second day on the job, I had blisters on both hands from the shavings of sheet metal, off the drill press. I was informed that no one was allowed to wear gloves because of the safety hazard of possibly getting the glove caught in the drill press, and therefore losing a hand. The second day, I managed to complete one drum and I made it to the acid room. However, I did not get a lunch or break because it was time to go home.

On the second day, more than two hundred people had quit. By the third day, more than half of the new employees had quit. This was a job where every person had a specific role in building a starter or alternator. If one person was slow then it held up production in another area. There was no flexibility, and the automation were set on high to produce more pieces in a given hour than normal. After four days of working in a hot warehouse with blisters on both of my hands, I listened to the supervisor yelling at all new employees that it was her way or the highway.

At the end of the fourth day, I had overheard two supervisors talking. I discovered the female supervisor had turned the automation on high, on purpose. It was to weed out the weak from the strong employees.

On the fifth day, there were only five hundred employees left. I had yet to take one break or get a lunch. When noon came around, I just stopped working and started walking away from the drill press that was on high speed. The female supervisor immediately yelled at me to get back to my station. I told her I needed a restroom break and lunch, and I kept walking. As I walked past her, she was still screaming at the top of her lungs that if I walked away from her and did not keep working, I was fired.

I took my restroom break and my lunch. When I went back to the drill press and my station, the female supervisor was standing there, doing my job. She said if I ever pulled that stunt again, I would be fired. Of course, I informed her I was reporting her to the Dept. of Labor, and I walked out, along with about fifty other people who witnessed the entire incident. This company was strictly focused on profit and efficient processes of manufacturing the starters and alternators. The managers were not flexible and did not care about their people. Once someone was shown how to do their job, they were expected to do just that, without complaints, breaks, or discussion.

This company, and all their managers were taking heat from the owners, who were only concerned about the bottom dollar. The managers thought they were being effective in training new employees and managing the different departments, however, with the dominating attitudes and disrespect towards the workers, they could not retain people. They might be weeding out the weak from the strong employees and this process was just repeated every week and every month, but they also were losing valuable people. It was a vicious cycle. The long-term consequences to the manager's communication approach eventually ruined the company's reputation and the company closed.

There was not any technology involved as far as communication. The managers just yelled across the warehouse to each other and to the employees. The scientific method of communication used at this facility was caveman style. In the beginning of hire, I needed the job. I had never worked for a manufacturing company before, especially one that had poor managers. The lack of respect to the employees was horrific and not acceptable to me. I tolerated it for five days because I wanted to give them the benefit of the doubt. Perhaps everyone was under stress because the plant just opened, and they had to produce a certain amount the first month to obtain contracts worldwide. However, the management style was lacking in every capacity. The executive leadership was out of country. The scientific method is still around today with a lot of companies focusing on specific tasks to be completed in a designated amount of time, along with strict enforcement of company policy (Hynes, & Veltsos, 2019). In a lot of these types of environments, you can find discrimination of all kinds, along with possible slave labor. It is unfortunate, but reality.

In the early nineteen eighties, I also worked for the prison system. The prison system is responsible for maintaining the safety of the community. They do this by protecting us from the criminals that have committed crimes and are incarcerated in the facilities. I worked in many departments within the agency. The communication system of the prison system was strictly administrative management style. All employees were expected to obey without question. If there were issues, the employee had a form that had to be completed and submitted to their immediate supervisor. If the supervisor felt it had merit, that person had to sign off on it and forward it up the chain of command. Sometimes, it was stopped before it ever left a department, because a supervisor did not want to bring any negative response to his/her dept. A lot of things have changed for the better in the past forty years. I believe this was strictly because of the excellent leadership over the past forty years. It takes time to create positive change, especially in an organization as large as this.

In the early 1980's, a friend of mine was hired as a correctional officer in a medium security prison. Her supervisor put her on the toughest row of inmates to monitor. She had complained to me about being the only correctional officer on that wing, and she was afraid. She was a woman amid violent male criminals. The inmates had a lot of time, where they were not on lock down but could walk around and do their assigned chores and activities. The agency was shorthanded by 30% and there was a hiring freeze. This reason alone is why there was only one guard posted on each wing. The policy stated there were to be always three to five guards at every post.

I talked to my supervisor directly about the dangers of putting a single female in a wing of the most violent criminals in that facility. My supervisor told me that danger comes with the job. I tried to go above my supervisor's head to her supervisor, but I was verbally chastised for not following protocol of filling out the form. I then filled out the complaint form, only to have it squashed again by my superior. Within a week of this occurring, my friend had gone to work and had just arrived at the post she was assigned to, when the inmates initiated a plan of escape.

During a twelve-hour riot, my friend was repeatedly raped and stabbed in the eye by a shank that an inmate had hidden. She lost one eye. She was only allowed to be off work for six weeks due to her injuries. When she returned to work, her supervisor put her on the exact same post she had prior to the attack. I voiced another complaint and again it was squashed by my supervisor. In the end, my friend ended up leaving employment with the prison system. She did not receive an opportunity to transfer to another job within the agency. The agency just accepted her resignation and went on about their business of finding someone else to work that post.

About a month after she left employment with the agency, I was in the elevator with the agency director one morning. I brought up the topic of my friend and how she had asked for help, and how I had asked for help, but my request had been squashed by my supervisor. The incident could have been prevented if the agency had placed more officers on the post with her. Because it was just a woman alone, the inmates saw this advantage and they took it, to escape the prison. The Director advised he never knew they only had one person on each post. That was against policy. It put employees at risk, and it also opened a door of opportunity for offenders to start a riot or escape. The chain of command is still in place at the agency, however, in cases such as this, it is considered an immediate threat and an employee can now bypass their immediate supervisor if that supervisor is not supportive of the request.

The administrative management system still exists today but with the help of electronics and computers, the turnaround time is much faster than forty years ago. In a way, both managers of both stories are the same as the employee was expected to do the work without question or complaint. There was not much technology in place in the early nineteen eighties. In both circumstances, the impact of communication was negative. The manufacturing company lost all their employees and had to close their doors. With the prison system, they lost a valuable and tenured employee because the chain of command was too long. The immediate supervisors stopped the complaint from ever leaving their dept. Neither of the two managers were effective in performing their responsibilities because they lost employees. The potential long-term consequences were loss of employees and also putting employees in danger of being hurt.

My position on the topic of the above communication theories remains firm. There needs to be open communication flowing from both directions between employee and manager. The one-sided communication is like a dictatorship. Times have changed. If you are leadership for these types of communication, you have an opportunity to create positive change within your organization.

The scientific method of communicating is a one-way communication example. The employee is expected to do as they are told without questioning and there is zero tolerance for policy violations. The administrative method of communicating is very similar to the scientific method as employees are expected to do as they are told without question. However, they do have recourse if there are issues. They can file a complaint through the chain of command. The problem with this type of communication is the time it takes to get to the top decision makers. During that time, in this case, an employee was brutally raped and stabbed in the eye with a prison shank. Employees can get hurt in the time it takes for a decision maker to make a decision. In my opinion, neither of these methods of communication are good.

Henri Fayol was responsible for developing the administrative theory (Uzuegbu, & Nnadozie, 2015) where discipline was an integral part of this communication theory. Every employee was to obey the rules and regulations of the leaders in the organization without question. However, with the global age we are now in, communication is made more concise and convenient through the internet. The internet has revolutionized the way of communicating in the business world (Soares, 2018). Times have indeed changed over the past forty years. In a matter of seconds, a top leader can be informed of serious incidents and can immediately initiate proper communication to all levels.

Yes, times have certainly changed. Granted, there are still dictatorship styles of communication management around the world, for the most part, leaders are realizing how ineffective this is. When leadership is open for direct communication, employees feel empowered and motivated to find solutions to problems, support leadership, and are more loyal. In this age of leadership, organizations are striving to be the best in their field, recruit and retain the best of the best employees. They are doing this by getting to know their employees and creating a culture of openness between leadership and staff based upon mutual respect and alignment of organizational goals.

Chapter 36 – Gender Communication

Gender can impact business communications within each country's workplace environment in many ways. In the year of 2016. the global import/export business for the United States passed two trillion dollars (Hynes & Veltsos, pg.333, 2019). The United States has been on a steady growth of involvement within the global scene. A lot of this has to do with the technology age and how fast things change and improve. The digital and electronic capabilities the USA have now makes it easier and quicker to network around the world in business. The USA is getting stronger every day because other countries want to invest in the USA.

With more and more trade agreements being signed, more global corporations are coming onto USA soil and bringing jobs here for our citizens. There might be a time when jobs might send a person to their parent country to conduct business. In addition, with the immigration increase in our country which accounts for almost fifty percent of the workforce (Hynes & Veltsos, pg.335, 2019), many managers find themselves working with a diverse workforce.

In Hofstede's Dimensions of Cultural Differences there are six different levels of culture around the globe. The Masculine/Feminine cultures describe a country's values and compares them to masculine or feminine. For example, if a country values money and assertiveness and things, then it would be considered a masculine culture. If a woman was hired into a masculine culture, her personal values might impact the way that country lives that is different than her own. Feminine cultures value family, children, and the quality of the lives of all, above money, and things (Hynes & Veltsos, pg. 338, 2019). If an aggressive salesperson is sent to a country that has a more feminine culture, he might not be received well from those in the workplace in that country.

Also, in some countries, women do not participate in business. In fact, in some countries, a woman cannot be seen holding hands and walking down a street, as it is offensive (Hynes & Veltsos, pg. 345, 2019) A good manager will be someone who can appreciate the differences among cultures and build strong relationships by not being judgmental or offensive. A leader that wants to learn about others in the workplace will help that manager embrace the changes and differences between them. Everyone can learn from each other and whether male or female. If a manager is respectful and empathetic and appears genuine to the people in that country and workplace, it will be easier to adapt to the environment.

In today's business environment to be successful, a manager needs to have a global mindset. Women are found to have more empathy and openness to diversity and are more diplomatic when it comes to other cultures and countries. Men are found to be more interpersonal and can appreciate the cosmopolitan outlook with a more business mindset (Javidan, Bullough & Dibble, 2016). It would be smart to send a male and female employee together to other countries to represent a corporation, to balance out the masculine/feminine cultural differences.

In ongoing environmental conflicts in countries where gender matters such as Africa and Iran, societies are struggling for ways to bring peace to these nations. It could be a perfect opportunity for nations to change their state laws and find new meaning for gender roles that could become a whole societal change (Frohlich & Gioli, 2015). In many parts of Africa and Iran women cannot own land or water. There are many organizations working to bring gender equality to these countries, however, when these cultures have behaved in certain ways for thousands of years, change is not welcome. It will take time to bring change regarding gender equality to some parts of the world. As the world is becoming more and more open to global trade and business, it will slowly evolve, and gender issues will hopefully become a thing of history.

Chapter 37 – Reiki/Tai Chi/Qi Gong/Yoga

The latest research conducted by the federal government shows people have spent more than 30.2 billion dollars a year on integrative therapy. Many people of the western culture have embraced eastern spiritual cultures of healing. Reiki (pronounced ray-key) is an eastern belief that vital energy flows through our bodies. Our bodies are made up of energy. Energy flows through our bodies system such as lymph, nerves, blood, and meridian pathways. Reiki is a Japanese energy technique that promotes relaxation, relieves stress, and anxiety. Because it focuses on the whole body, (mind, body, and emotions) it can be successful in all types of physical, emotional, mental, and spiritual healing.

Tai Chi and Qi Gong are two Chinese martial arts practiced for health benefits, meditation, and even defense training. Both forms improve strength, flexibility, aerobic conditioning, and balance within the body. It has been proven to improve cardiovascular fitness, lower blood pressure, prevent falls, and even help people who have arthritis. The American Osteopathic Association compares Tai Chi to yoga as having the same benefits. Tai Chi combines physical exercise, breathing, meditation, lifestyle change and philosophical awareness of the world. Qi Gong is very similar to Tai Chi but is more focused on a single movement. Tai Chi is a series of movements that work on the whole body.

According to the National Institute of Health, scientific evidence shows yoga supports stress management, mental health, mindfulness, healthy eating, weight loss, and quality sleep (NIH, 2022). John Hopkins Medicine lists nine benefits of yoga on their website (www.hopkinsmedicine.org). The U.S. military, the National Institute of Health and many other large organizations are embracing scientific validation of the value of including yoga in health care. Many communities offer yoga for seniors. The important thing to remember, is you can advance at your own pace. Many people find it helps with balance issues, oncology, chronic pain, women's health, osteopenia, arthritis, mindfulness, relaxation, depression, mood, and stress. Many organizations offer yoga as part of their new wellness plans.

Chapter 38 – Reflexology

Reflexology is based upon the Chinese belief in Qi (pronounced Chee), or vital energy. According to Chinese belief, whenever the body feels stress, then it blocks the natural flow of energy. This causes an imbalance in the human body and can also lead to many chronic illnesses. In the late 1890's, scientists from Britain discovered that nerves in the human body connect the skin and internal organs. They also discovered the body's entire nervous system tends to respond to outside factors, including touch.

Reflexology is a massage integrative therapy of the feet, hands, or ears, focusing on specific pressure points. This type of therapy can calm the nervous system, promoting relaxation and other benefits like any other form of massage. There is eastern reflexology and there is western reflexology. According to traditional Chinese medicine (TCM), reflexology promotes better sleep, reduces stress, aids in digestion, and can pinpoint health issues in different parts of the body. The theory behind reflexology is that each pressure point coincides with specific systems and organs in the body. It can even be used to stimulate the endocrine and nervous system (https://www.mayoclinic.org).

Reflexology is also helpful in flushing out toxins from the body by stimulating the energy flow through the important organs that are involved in detoxification such as the liver, kidneys, skin, lungs, and colon. My experience with reflexology has been very enlightening. I have found with western reflexology the therapists will ease up on the pressure if the client feels pain in a specific area. The Chinese reflexology focuses on the pain and will even increase the pressure to stimulate that area. It can be very relaxing, and it can also be very painful if you have health issues. However, upon saying that, I noticed a drastic difference in improvement after receiving the Chinese reflexology therapy. Personally, the western reflexology was more of a foot massage at best. The Chinese reflexology was extremely healing to me. I am sure, it will depend on the therapist you find. Most of reflexologists are certified.

There are not many scientific studies out there on reflexology. In 2011, a study funded by the National Cancer Institute focused on two hundred and forty women who had advanced breast cancer. All the women were undergoing chemotherapy of some sort at the time of the study. The results showed it helped in reducing some of their symptoms, including shortness of breath (www.ncbi.nlm.nih.gov). Research is ongoing for treatment of PMS in women, stress, and anxiety.

For the most part, reflexology is very noninvasive and safe, even for people who have serious health issues. It is important to discuss it first with your physician if you have serious health issues including issues such as bruising or bleeding easily, open wounds, blood clots, fungal infections, pregnant, or even circulatory issues of the feet. The physician can determine if the reflexology is a good complimentary therapy for you to try.

Chapter 39 – Massage Therapy

Massage therapy is used to help people relax and reduce anxiety by manipulating the muscles and soft tissue. A physical therapist is a person who works with clients that have specific injuries like fractures. There are three types of massage: Swedish massage, Deep Tissue massage, and Sports massage. The Swedish massage is the most common type that people request because of the longer and softer strokes the therapists use to relax the muscles and increase blood flow to the area.

The Deep Tissue massage is used when a client has a particular issue such as a stiff neck or knot in the back or shoulder area. This type of massage focuses on specific areas of the body to relieve painful situations. The therapist will apply deeper and more intense pressure to the layers of the muscles and tissue in the problem areas. This type of massage often uses a transverse friction method which is an oscillating pressure across the direction of tissue for tendons and ligament injuries. If you have sensitive skin issues, this type of massage might be painful to you.

The Sports massage is used for sport injuries or sprains and strains of specific muscles. Athletes often use this type of massage prior to activity, during a sports event, and even after a sports event. Many athletes rely on sports massages to facilitate healing of specific muscles and tendons.

Chapter 40 – Functional Food

In the late nineteen eighties, the term functional food was first developed in Japan. The nation's health organizations were searching for ways to support the wellbeing of their aging population.

Functional foods are foods that are rich in antioxidants, nutrients, and help strengthen the body's ability to fight disease. These molecules help neutralize harmful compounds like free radicals, helping prevent damage to cells and many chronic illnesses, including diabetes, cancer, and heart disease. Functional foods contain antioxidants such as lycopene, polyphenols, flavonoids, and carotenoids, that can help fight inflammation, support healthy guts, enhance the immune system, and even provide important live microbial cultures called probiotic bacteria.

In the United States, the Food and Drug Administration does not regulate use of the term "functional food". Therefore, you must be very careful when you purchase products that claim it is a functional food or offers functional food benefits. There are a lot of misleading health claims on processed foods. Many products claim they are fortified and enriched food. The fortified and enriched food products are not the same as functional food. There are many meal replacement shakes, cereal grains and juices on the market today called nutraceuticals that claim to be enriched. These are not functional foods. Functional foods naturally possess phytonutrients, antioxidants, and many other helpful compounds.

These natural ingredients help balance a body's sugar levels, help build and maintain bone mass, help maintain weight management, help balance cholesterol levels, helps support detoxification and good gut health, and even helps fight stress by providing B vitamins, omega 3 fatty acids, and magnesium. Functional foods also help protect the brain from free radicals and supports healthy cognitive functions.

The best functional foods are whole foods. These are live fruits and vegetables. The foods that contain high antioxidants include brightly colored fruits and vegetables like bell peppers, oranges, papaya, blueberries, raspberries, leafy greens, goji, acai, cranberries, brussel sprouts, broccoli, sweet potatoes, and carrots. Green foods such as sea vegetables and grasses contain nutrients that are hard to find. Examples of these types of foods are wheat grass, barley, spirulina, and chlorella. Foods that contain high fiber are excellent for gut health. High fiber can be found in avocados, beans, whole grains, nuts, vegetables, and fresh fruit.

When looking to add probiotic foods to your diet, you can look for Greek yogurt, fermented foods like sauerkraut and kimchi. It is important to add probiotic foods to your diet as it helps protect the lining of the gastrointestinal tract and helps ward off infections.

When adding prebiotic foods to your diet, you can look for carbohydrates/fibers such as bananas, onions, garlic, asparagus, oatmeal, potatoes, artichokes, and leeks. When a person eats raw plant foods, it is one of the best ways to introduce natural digestive enzymes into the system.

Foods that contain Omega 3 fatty acids include wild caught fish like salmon, mackerel, halibut, and fresh nuts like walnuts, and seeds like flax and chia. Eating Omega 3 fatty acid foods are great for supporting healthy brain function, may reduce depression, inflammation, and heart disease.

Foods that are high in fiber include nuts like cashew, almonds, walnuts, and chia seeds. These types of natural foods can help curb hunger between meals and aid in weight loss. They contain healthy fats and can aid in brain and heart health.

A lot of fresh teas, herbs are highly beneficial due to their antioxidant contents. Fresh herbs add flavor to a lot of meals without adding calories. Green tea, ginger, cinnamon, turmeric, and black tea are only a few foods that offer high anti-inflammatory and antimicrobial benefits. Dark chocolate, raw cocoa and red wine also can be called functional foods because they are very high in phytonutrients.

Bone broth is another functional food that is very dense in amino acids, which help develop proteins like glycine, arginine, and proline. Bone broth is very high in vitamins, collagen, minerals, electrolytes and has antioxidants like glucosamine.

To keep a healthy body, it is good to focus on plant-based diets. If you do eat a lot of animal proteins such as eggs, dairy, meat, then try to buy grass fed, cage free, wild caught foods, and pasture raised because these are higher in nutrients are less likely to contain hormones or other harmful additives. It is also better to have whole grains than processed flour. It helps promote good gut health if you stay away from processed foods, sugar of all kinds, refined carbohydrates, corn, and soybean oils, pasteurized dairy products, trans fats, and processed grains.

Many organizations offer fresh fruit and vegetables during meetings instead of donuts and processed foods filled with sugar. It takes discipline to stay on a healthy food regime. Everyone struggles and everyone makes choices. Don't beat yourself up if you get off track. Just get back on. It is a lifestyle change and often takes time to create a permanent change.

I would also like to say if you are living in an area where fresh foods are limited, then focus on frozen foods over canned products. Many frozen foods are flash frozen upon picking from the fields or vines. These are healthier than most canned foods you purchase in the store. People living in remote areas often buy bulk fresh vegetables and fruit and either freeze the products or opt for canning process. This way, the person knows what is in the jar of vegetables or fruit and most often is only added water. It is also even more ideal if you can grow your own vegetables and fruit, either in a greenhouse or on your property. If you have never tried this, the internet has literally thousands of how-to videos or books to learn by.

The bottom line, our body is the only one we have. It makes sense to take care of it. It is important to ask yourself before you eat something, whether that food is going to feed wellness into your body or feed illness.

Chapter 41 – Global Wellness/PTSD/Trauma

Around the world, manmade disasters such as war, genocide, terrorism, and also natural disasters such as Tsunamis, hurricanes, volcanic activity, to only name a few, have caused post-traumatic stress disorders, anxiety, stress, and trauma in all age groups, gender, ethnicity, and cultures. There are over one hundred and twenty clinical trials that talk about energy psychology and how it has been applied in more than thirty countries for victims of catastrophic events (David Feinstein, 2022).

Energy psychology is the manual stimulation of acupuncture points with imaginal exposure, cognitive restructuring, and other evidence-based psycho-therapeutic procedures. There are four tiers of intervention. The first tier is the most important in providing immediate psychological relief after a catastrophic event. The other three tiers of therapy are followed up over time, as chronic disorders develop. Psychological effects of catastrophic events include depression, anger, shock, substance abuse, despair, insecurity, and grief. These types of effects have been found to most severe in children, the elderly, and women.

Disasters come and go, but the recovery time is usually over a long period of time. Mental health workers began responding to natural disasters in the late nineteen nineties. Today, it is more advanced and well thought out. Mental health teams will work closely with disaster relief teams. It takes everyone working together to bring help to those in need.

In leadership, this is one reason it is important to get to know your employees. A person is more than what you can see. A person never knows where a person has lived, what experiences they have endured, or what trauma they have been exposed to. It takes nothing to be a kind human being to another. It takes time to build strong relationships and strong teams. It begins with respect and kindness.

Chapter 42 – Energy Psychology-Tapping

Tapping is a method of energy psychology. It focuses on the manual stimulation of acupuncture points with imaginal exposure, cognitive restructuring, and other evidence-based psycho-therapeutic procedures, by tapping with fingers. It is used for emotional healing in victims of catastrophic events. Energy psychology and other somatic interventions have been referred to as the "fourth wave" of psychotherapy, following psychoanalysis, behavior therapy, and cognitive approaches (Stapleton, P., 2019). It is estimated there are "tens of thousands" of therapists practicing energy psychology techniques (Leskowitz, E. 2016). The technique of tapping has been particularly promising due to its ability to regulate the physiological aftermath of an event, providing immediate relief and stabilization (Feinstein, D., 2022).

In the past, mental health assistance has been neglected during traumatic events. The focus has been on immediate physical and economic recovery. However, traumatic events can disrupt entire communities and cause many dysfunctional problems. There are many people who can continue to function normally after a traumatic event. Others, however, may need crisis counseling, sometimes for years.

This is a great area to add to the wellness program. There are several programs available that teach the tapping techniques. Often, small business owners do not have the extra funds to create big wellness programs and feel left out. This would be training that is affordable for the small business owner and very beneficial during a crisis, not only in an organization, but in your community.

The Center for Mind-Body Medicine in Washington, DC. was one of the very first organizations to bring mind-body interventions into post disaster deployment. They have been offering their programs for over thirty years and research is continuing to this day (Feinstein, D., 2022).

Chapter 43 – Wellness Checks

In the United States, a wellness check is usually associated with law enforcement. If you or someone you know is concerned about the welfare or mental health of a person or children, you can call and request law enforcement to perform what is called a wellness check. They usually drop in to ensure the person or children are safe and not in any type of danger. Many wellness checks have saved lives. A request for a wellness check can be anonymous. It is critical to relay information as you know it to law enforcement, so their response can be planned according to the situation.

Years ago, as I worked for the State of Oklahoma Department of Corrections, I was talking with a parolee in the office. During the conversation, I noticed how distraught he was. He kept talking about how his wife had left him, taking his children, and moving out of state. He repeatedly spoke about thoughts of suicide. After about thirty minutes, it was obvious the man was asking for help. I notified my superior officer and they called for assistance from local law enforcement. I felt bad when they took him, but I know he was transferred to a local mental health facility for evaluation and help. If I had not called for help, and something happened, I would have felt worse for not being of assistance when someone was in need. In cases such as these, you must decide.

Another instance, I experienced years ago, was with a family member. I received a phone call and the person on the other end was so distraught, I could barely understand the words they were saying. What I did hear was "I am thinking of killing myself". I was forty miles away. I immediately told them I would come, and I needed them to wait for me, so we could talk it out and I could help. As soon as I hung up the phone, I contacted my local law enforcement and after relaying the situation, they contacted the local law enforcement in that city. I drove my car as fast as I could, up to this family member's house, only to find the person sitting on the front step, smiling, and smoking a cigarette with a policeman. When I got out of the car, the person was livid with me, saying "can't a person have a bad hair day?". I was very appreciative of the fast response of law enforcement. However, I felt like a jackass. But I would do the same again, if needed. I would have felt bad if I had not responded as I had, and something had happened. I guess, it was a lesson learned. It is important to pay attention to gut feelings about a situation. All situations are different and may require different responses.

Chapter 44 – Meditation

The art of meditation has been practiced for thousands of years. It was originally used to help understand the meaning of life. In today's world, it is a technique that can reduce anxiety and stress by finding a sense of calm within. It is considered a mind-body complementary medicine. It can be done anywhere, anytime, and does not cost a thing.

When a person is under high stress or anxiety, they can focus their attention on something calming, therefore, eliminating the stressful situation at hand. Practicing meditation can be very healthy and promote a sense of calm and peace in your life. Meditation can also help in emergency medical situations to bring a sense of calm. Meditation should not be used in replacement of medical attention but can be very helpful as a complementary technique.

There are many types of meditation that bring the same relaxed state of being. Guided meditation is when a person focuses on visualization of mental pictures of places or situations that you feel are very relaxing. Many guided meditations include music, sounds of water, animals, and stories.

Mantra meditation is when a person silently repeats a phrase or word that brings them focus and calm. This type of meditation can be helpful when your mind is full of distracting thoughts or problems.

Mindful meditation is having an acute awareness of living in the present moment. By broadening your conscious awareness, you focus on the moment, the feelings, the experience, without judgment.

Qi Gong is part of traditional Chinese medicine and combines meditation, relaxation, with physical movements and breathing exercises. Tai Chi is also a part of traditional Chinese medicine that incorporates gentle breathing, postures, movements to bring a peaceful state. It is also a form of martial art.

Yoga is a form of meditation that concentrates on specific body movements and balance. The movements and balance require a person to focus on that instead of things that are going on in your life. Many people find yoga is very relaxing and reduces anxiety and stress.

Meditation requires a quiet place, a comfortable position, relaxed breathing, and focused attention. There are many organizations that offer quiet places for employees to regroup or unwind during the day. Some organizations offer yoga classes before work or after work.

There are many resources if you are interested in learning more about meditation. The one thing to remember is there is not a right or wrong way to meditate. You just must find what works best for you. Some people can meditate while taking a walk by themselves. This can even occur during your workday or lunch hour. It helps to get your mind calm and in a relax state of mind, so you can focus on other issues later.

Chapter 45 – Culture

It is the leader's responsibility to create a healthy culture of an organization. When employees feel empowered and inspired, they will become more loyal, more productive, and feel more valued.

Leadership is a big responsibility. Everything a leader does affects the people around him/her. A manager has the authority to make decisions. These decisions can be good, or they can be bad. As a leader, managers must be mindful of how their actions will affect those around them. Good leaders always take responsibility for all their actions and hold themselves to the highest accountability. When a leader makes decisions that affect the people around him/her, then the leadership develops an ethical dimension. It is the responsibility of a leader to teach and develop his employees. This can be done amid change. Change can be difficult for employees and leaders alike. It is during the toughest of changes, employees need to see their leaders as examples of strength, courage, caring and helpful (Manning & Curtis, 2019). Leaders must have high expectations of themselves and all those who follow. A positive attitude is also crucial to developing the employees into leaders themselves.

Leaders have the power to transform every employee for the better. When a leader sets the example themselves, and sets the bar higher than normal, people will learn by this and follow the leader's example. It is important for a leader to ensure the resources are available to be successful. Every employee appreciates feedback that lets them know how they are doing and how they can improve even more. When an employee needs corrective action, it is important to do it at the time and not wait. It is easier to redirect an employee than to undo six months of errors. It is empowering when a leader acknowledges and rewards employees for a job well done. Employees will gain self-esteem when they are encouraged by someone they respect (Manning & Curtis, 2019).

It is always critical that a leader respect and value all persons and their dignity. Every person learns differently. Leaders and employees can learn together and find ways to see other's viewpoints and ways of doing things that are different than their own. Leaders who are coaches will receive higher levels of productivity from employees (Manning & Curtis, 2019). It is important for managers and leaders to get to know their employees and develop a strong relationship with them. Employees who have a relationship with their leaders will find it easier to communicate with them during challenging times. Organizations will go through many changes during its lifespan. It is during these changes that leaders and employees both need to be flexible and willing to change. Employees should have a positive attitude and a willingness to invest in themselves. Personal development becomes an asset with an employee who is not too old to learn.

Employees want to see their leaders walking the talk. They expect leaders to have a strong vision they can follow and use as a guideline to success. During the toughest of times, leaders' ethical values will shine. Leaders need to be strong and confront other managers who do not support the needed changes. They always need to express clear and concise communication. Many leaders emerge, through challenging times, even stronger. They become stress resistant, and their actions become more mindful with integrity and wholeness (Manning & Curtis, 2019).

Virginia Rometty, of IBM, was a leader who empowered her people. She made sure they had confidence in their own knowledge and skills to make important decisions. She created a safe environment for all employees. Employees of IBM knew they could be innovative and creative with new technology. If something did not work like they thought it might, they went back to the drawing board, and worked together as a team. They were not afraid of losing their jobs. They knew they had the support of the entire leadership. A great leader is a leader who can empower his/her employees and encourage them to try new things (Kifer, Heler, Perunovic, & Galinsky, 2013).

To become a great leader, it is important to empower people to become better and great themselves. When teams are empowered to work together, they gain self-confidence and the skills needed to succeed. These types of teams do not fear of sharing ideas and creativity. They boldly blend with diversified groups of people to become stronger and create amazing things in whatever field they are in. When a leader values the people that work for him/her, then it creates a servant leadership style that sets the tone for generations of future leaders to emulate. Employees who feel valued by their leaders will increase their productivity and the job satisfaction rate will rise (McNeff & Irving, 2017). Employees will strive to become better, not only as an individual, but as a society. This is the type of leadership legacy that should be left behind. This is transformational leadership.

IBM is a great example of transformational leadership. IBM is a very innovative and progressive company. They live what they believe. Their values and vision are supported by every employee and every department of the company. In IBM, they have created a culture of health because it is the very foundation of every decision in the company. They support what is called the five dimensions of health. This is physical, mind, financial, social and purpose. They believe these five dimensions affect the well-being of the body mind and every relationship the person has. Therefore, IBM supports employees aligning their values with their work and life. IBM has a strong commitment to its employees, its customers, and stakeholders. They believe their ability to help their customers depends on the overall well-being of every employee (IBM, 2020)

Every employee is inspired to be better and to perform better. All employees are aligned and on the same path and vision of IBM. It is evident the leaders of the company believe the vision and tone of the organization as they support every single person with the agency. The basic three motivations for leadership are: power, achievement, and affiliation (Manning & Curtis, 2019). These leaders of IBM believe in the company and what they are doing. They are helping others and making a difference in the lives of millions of people around the world.

Overall, IBM has a strong and clear vision. It supports its employees and customers in any way it can be progressive. For the most part, it has evolved into positive changes for the world. IBM has held strong moral and ethical values for almost one hundred years. They empower every one of their employees and partners to be better every day. They build strong relationships and encourage innovation which builds self-esteem in employees and people they partner with. They encourage employees to admit their failures along with their successes and learn from them.

IBM has been a leader in ethical business practices for over one hundred years. They were the first company to provide life insurance, survivor benefits, and paid vacation to employees during the entire depression era (IBM, 2014). They continue to be socially responsible in everything they do. They encourage employees and empower everyone that encounters IBM. They also only do business with partners around the world that hold the same corporate ethical standards. This is difficult to do, especially in the mineral torn countries like Africa and India.

It is important to be a great leader, but not as important as it is to leave a great legacy of leadership. Leadership is not always about a title or responsibilities. It is about what kind of person the leader is, not only at work, but every single day. It is nice to have strategic ideas to share with employees and others, but this is not what people will remember about a great leader. What legacy a great leader leaves behind after they are long gone will be demonstrated by how employees think and behave, and how they approach life in general because they learned from a great leader. All in all, IBM is this type of leader. With over nine thousand patents in the year 2019 alone, the Watson artificial intelligence of 2012 will be one of the biggest legacies left behind that changed the world for the better. It is the hope of this author that IBM continues to invest their billions of dollars into more research and engineering of the Watson AI unit and return to the world, a product they promised.

Chapter 46 – Workplace Environments

Workplace environments set the tone for the whole organization. This includes the outside environment, the individual offices, the break rooms, the quiet spaces, rest rooms, meeting rooms, work areas, and people. There are so many issues that can make or break a workplace environment. These issues range from clean quality air in the facilities to clutter and unsafe work conditions, to toxic employees.

Ask yourself, what kind of culture does your organization have? Is it healthy? Is it toxic? Is leadership transparent with all employees? Is the environment a safe environment where people are free to ask questions and provide thoughts and ideas for innovation? How do you value diversity in the workplace? Does the organization welcome minorities? Does the organization welcome different cultures? Do your employees feel valued and respected? Is the environment a clean environment? What kind of healthy snacks and food does your workplace offer?

Is the human resource department filled with capable people? What kind of career development program do you have? What kind of employee assistance program do you have in place? If you had a problem, would you go to the HR department for help? Do you support wellness in the workplace? If so, are you involved in any of the programs yourself?

If you have thousands of employees and feel it is impossible to get to know them. Get to know your immediate employees. Teach your people to teach their people and all the way down the line, to value everyone. Create the type of culture needed to empower and inspire everyone. Become transparent and share your vision. Look at your employees and begin developing top talent for future leaders within the organization. Start investing in your people to create the best employee workforce ever.

Agency wide surveys are a great tool to get a pulse of your organization. Ask pointed questions of what needs to change, what tools do the employees need to do their jobs, what kind of ideas do they have for wellness in the workplace. Create a place for people to either mail it back or drop into a box. Make the survey anonymous, so people will be free to speak their minds.

People are struggling to get back into the workforce after COVID. A lot of organizations are struggling with lack of employees and people are having to pick up the slack. It will take a while for things to balance out, but everything comes full circle. It is a cycle of nature. Now, more than ever, people need to be supported in every aspect. Do what you can do to make the environment a healthy one for everyone.

Chapter 47 – Mindfulness

Mindfulness is about slowing down. Look around you. Everyone is in such a hurry. They are in a hurry to get up in the morning. They are in a hurry to get to work. They are in a hurry to each lunch. They are in a hurry to get through the day. They are in a hurry to mark everything off their to do list and get home. People are in such a hurry; nothing is enjoyable anymore.

Being mindful begins with you. When you wake up in the morning, lay there for a minute or two or three. Feel your breathing and become aware of your body. Think about how you feel. Savor that moment before you truly must put your feet on the floor and get up. Think about what you are most grateful for. For me, it is waking up every morning that fills me with gratitude for another day. I then, think about what I want to accomplish on this day alone. I think about what might make my day a little better. I also think about what would make me happy. This puts a smile on my face, and I start the day on the right foot.

Take today, for example. I woke up early. I took my time getting up and around, enjoying my time with my cats. I then, thought about what I had in store for myself. I am going to take three of my grandchildren to school and back for the next three days. It is a treat. It makes me happy to spend time with all my grandchildren and when I have the opportunity to help, I jump on it.

I also thought about what would make me happy today. So, I have deliberately set aside four hours to write and four hours to paint. This is in and around spending time with and driving my grandchildren to and from school today.

When it comes to mindfulness, it is about being deliberate with every move you make. It is savoring every bite of food you put into your mouth and enjoying your meal. It is about finding joy in preparing your meal if you cook. There have been times, when I was in such a hurry, I do not even remember what I ate. I ate so fast and ate only what I could grab at that moment. I used to drive on the freeway, an extra ten to fifteen miles over the speed limit because I was always in a hurry to get somewhere. I never developed road rage like some people I know. That is one thing I am grateful for.

Being mindful is about being present in the moment. When I sit down at a meal with my husband, I sit across from him so

I can look directly at him and have a conversation. I enjoy the moments together, even if it is at a meal. There was a time, when we both worked eighty hours a week, we were in such a hurry about everything. When we ate a meal together, neither one of us spoke a word because we were so busy gulping down our food. And, what for? Just so we could go back to work. There comes a time when you realize life does fly by and we are not even paying attention. Then, you realize, you are sixty, seventy, eighty years old.

When you learn the art of mindfulness, you will engage with your family, your friends, your coworkers, your employees better. You will walk away from them feeling like you shared a moment.

As a leader, being mindful is about thinking things through before you meet with an employee or businessperson. It is important to think about what you want to share, how you want to share it, and what would bring you joy in that moment. This sets the tone before you ever walk into a room to meet with that person. It is not to say, the meeting is scheduled to be a termination or other upsetting meeting. In those circumstances, you do have to be mindful of how you want to react if the meeting goes south. Chances are, if you go into the meeting with a mindfulness attitude, the meeting will go well.

Our subconscious minds usually run our lives. This is why we say and do things sometimes, we are not sure where it comes from. Well, it comes from you. It comes from the deepest part of your heart and mind. This is also why it is important to pull out all the old trauma, pain, issues you may have buried years ago and just deal with it. When you do this, it helps you to move forward in a positive way without worrying about hidden anger or grief popping up at inappropriate times. I am not saying it won't ever do this, but it will be less frequent, for sure.

There are many online web sites that give guidance on how to be mindful. They are great. Carve out some time and listen to some of them. Some are tied to meditation. Some are just great ideas on how to get started with being present in every aspect of your life. It truly slows you down to where you can enjoy every moment.

Adding mindfulness classes to your new employee wellness center is a great idea. It will help your employees learn how to slow down, enjoy what they do, be more creative, more involved, more appreciative, and more in tune with their own lives. It is such a positive thing to teach others.

Chapter 48 – Gratitude

I used to take everyone and everything for granted. These days, I am grateful I have a home. I am grateful I woke up to another day. I am grateful for my family, my friends, and all the opportunities that are ahead of me. Life has a way of humbling you. It humbles us all.

Gratitude is about being thankful and expressing that emotion. It can be something simple or something bigger. When we express our gratitude to somebody for something they did or said, it makes for positive interactions between people. We relish those moments in our lives. It is often the smallest of things we remember, long after someone is gone. Being grateful improves not only our health, but the health of others. We can use it to deal with adversity. When bad things happen, we can immediately focus on the things the experience leaves us with or has taught us. If you look hard enough, you can find the lesson in every experience and be grateful for what it teaches you.

Being grateful builds strong relationships. It can be as simple as my husband putting a load of clothes into the washing machine and stripping the bed and washing blankets for me. I am grateful for that every single week. We have been together for fifteen years. Right off the bat, he learned that laundry was not my favorite thing in the world. From that moment forward, he consciously chose to do the laundry and the weekly sheets and blanket chores. I am very grateful for this. It is one of those things that makes our relationship stronger. In return, I love to cook. I do not particularly care about washing dishes, but neither does he. So, I consciously choose to cook and clean the kitchen as my thing to do. For me, it is the least I can do if he does the laundry.

In the morning, one of the first things I do is think about all the things I am grateful for. It helps put a smile on my face and makes me happy. Therefore, my day is good. At the end of the day, before I go to sleep, I do it again. I think about all the things, unexpected that happened that day that made me grateful. I sleep better. I sleep more sound and I get much needed rest.

Being grateful improves your self-esteem and those to whom you are grateful to. Expressing gratitude can be as simple as saying thank you to someone for their kindness or deed. It takes hardly any time to be thankful and share that moment. It costs nothing. The benefits are great.

Being grateful also can help with adversity. When I worry about something I need to say to someone, I always start off with how grateful I am towards them. It sets the tone for the conversation. It helps build stronger relationships.

Gratitude can reduce stress, anxiety, burnout, symptoms of post-traumatic stress disorder (PTSD), increases resilience, and fosters a sense of hope for the future. Being grateful also can help with slowing down and savoring the moments of being present.

We can show gratitude by serving others, putting others first, and by being humble. Whenever we have a negative experience, negative thought, or are around negative people, showing gratitude can turn that into a positive experience. Around the holidays, there are a lot of people who are hurting, for a million different reasons. However, when we include these people or even show them, they are valued, it brings gratefulness to their door. Thinking about all the things that are going right and not focusing on all the things that might be going wrong, can calm a person. It can connect them with something bigger than themselves, in that moment.

In positive psychology research, gratitude is strongly and consistently associated with greater happiness. Gratitude helps people feel happier, more positive about life, improves their health, relish good experiences, and helps with adversity (Harvard, 2022).

This is a great opportunity for leadership to include courses on gratitude to their employees. It will be a feel-good day when all can learn how to incorporate gratitude into their lives. You will notice the vibes in the air change around the office when people actually take the time to be thankful to those who help or say something kind. It could be as simply thanking them for being present.

Chapter 49 -Fear-Unexpressed Emotions

Everybody holds onto feelings over their lifetime. It can be feelings of grief, feelings of anger, feelings of pain. Whatever they are, the body stores it. There is a definite connection between the human body, the human mind, and the human spirit. As we get older, we hold onto those feelings instead of sharing them out of fear what people might think of us. In the end, these negative feelings over time can cause not only stress, anxiety, depression, but can cause cancer.

I had several intense trauma experiences at ages three and four. When I was twenty-four, I discovered I had thyroid cancer in my throat. The tumor was determined to be twenty years old. If I had not gone in for a complete physical, my life might have ended by the time I turned twenty-five years old. It was that far advanced. I was grateful because thyroid cancer is the slowest growing cancer there is. I never smoked. I never did drugs. I was in great shape at the time, despite this. I spent the next thirty-five years trying to understand why I had cancer in my throat in the first place.

My journey took me to a lot of places I never even dreamed of going. In Alaska, I met with several Athabaskan (native Alaskan Indian) medicine healers. Upon returning from Alaska to Arkansas, I met with a Cherokee Medicine Man from Conway, Arkansas. I received the same message from all these people. I developed cancer and tumors in my throat because I held onto fear from childhood experiences. I was scared to death to speak. The pain and fear I needed to express was stuck in my throat. It really makes sense when I think about it. It was not until I began talking about the things, I was afraid of, that I began to heal. It was a slow process because I was still afraid to talk about them.

Over the past years, from the time I was diagnosed with the cancer, until today (I am 61 this week), my cancer would return almost like clockwork every ten years. I would have to stop what I was doing and deal with it every time. Since, 2005, I have been cancer free. It was in 2005 that I began talking about my unexpressed emotions and pain from my childhood. I truly believe there is a connection between the body, the mind, and the spirit.

Being grateful, showing gratitude, being mindful and present are things that help everyone. They can especially help any person that has experienced trauma of any kind. It might be from the war, it might be from domestic violence, it might be from bullying. The bottom line is we tend to suppress all negative emotions. They stay buried alive for a long time. For some people, they stay buried alive their entire life.

I am not a psychologist, psychiatrist, medical physician, or therapist. I am speaking from experience and how I held onto things my entire life, until I pulled the issues out and dealt with them. It is very painful. It is very healing. The weight that lifted off my shoulders was tremendous. I immediately felt better. I realized how much anger I held onto, along with fear and pain. They are ugly emotions and can do a lot of damage to yourself. Holding onto these types of emotions can cause a person to forget they deserve love, they deserve happiness, they deserve goodness. It makes it hard to give love also, even to your own family. Self-sabotage can kill you.

In leadership, I have seen superiors that had massive rage issues. They scared the hell out of everyone working for them. Employees made themselves scarce whenever these leaders came around. What kind of environment would you think that makes? Unhealthy. Some people need professional help to cope with suppressed emotions. Others can find alternative ways to deal with them.

I am sharing this experience only because I hope it can help someone else. If you, as a leader, have held onto suppressed emotions, take some time to deal with those issues. There is nothing shameful about taking care of your mind, body, and spirit. Don't let anyone make you think there is. You deserve a good, happy life, just as much as the next person. You will thank yourself.

Chapter 50 – Detox & Cleanse

Your skin is the largest organ you have. Twenty-four hours a day, it is absorbing toxins from the environment. These toxins make their way into your blood stream and other major organs. People who live in the city or close to it, have bigger issues because of the smog and pollution. I live in the country, and I have a few of my own. Over time, toxins build up and can cause all kinds of issues. For me, I became seriously allergic to almost everything. My body was fighting off other things, and normal things I loved to eat, soon became highly allergic.

Hygiene is extremely important. Everyone takes daily showers and brushes their teeth. Very few people think about keeping the dirt and junk out of the inside body. Wellness on the inside is just as important as wellness on the outside. It is important to learn about balancing out the body, mind, and spirit. There are many topics online about detox and cleansing the body. There are many facilities you can check out.

Many people regularly detox once a month. Some detox twice a year. One of the things I have learned over the past five years is how much juicing helps. I have several books on juicing. I have several juice machines. Since I have incorporated this into my lifestyle, my skin on my face is vibrant and healthy. I feel better on the inside. You can do the research and find what works best for you.

For me, I love taking a whole bag of carrots and two apples and drinking the pure live juice from that. I also have discovered celery juice. The organic celery I buy is fresh and has live enzymes in it. I will buy five bunches at a time. This lasts for five days and makes one serving a day. I will wash a whole bunch and juice a bunch each day. One whole bunch makes about eight ounces of juice each. The interesting thing about celery is it has natural salts in it. The juice goes directly into your bloodstream and the salts help clear out cholesterol and other junk in your blood stream. It goes on and does the same thing in your liver and your kidneys. When I juice celery every day, I feel great. I feel it cleanses out my insides naturally. I have less allergic reactions to food and the environment. I feel good. The first couple of days, the juice tasted bitter, but after that, I began to enjoy it. I also found there is a different taste between organic celery and regular celery. I buy the organic. It tastes sweeter and does not have any pesticides or chemicals on it.

Good health starts on the inside. It is about everything you feed your body, from food to your relationships, to your job. Good health does not happen overnight. It is a lifetime lifestyle change. Take it one day at a time and give yourself credit for taking the first step. When you are healthy, you are happier. Your family is happier. You have time and energy to do the things you want to do in life, outside of work.

As a leader, this is a great topic to add to the wellness center for you and your employees. There is a lot to learn about wellness on the inside. Don't be afraid to share it, because when a person is well on the inside, they are well on the outside. When people feel good, they are more productive, happier to be around, take less sick leave, and end up motivating others to be the best they can be.

Have you ever taken a good look at people's faces? If you look around, you will see people whose skin is bright and vibrant, while other's skin is gray and pale. You can tell who is healthy and who is not healthy. Be the example. Be the leader in whole body wellness. People will notice.

Chapter 51 – Whole Food Nutrition

Whole food nutrition is the best for your body. This is fresh fruits, fresh vegetables, fresh fish, and if you do eat meat, like I do, choose the grass fed or organic. It is a lifestyle change. Cut out anything that is processed. Cut out sugar. If you have a hard time cutting out sugar, change to a natural sugar. Something that is not processed like white sugar. I struggle with sugar. It is my biggest weakness. I like natural brown sugar in my oatmeal. I do not put near as much in it as I used to. I also have switched to natural honey. One teaspoon gives the sweetness I need, without all the other harmful chemicals that is attached to white sugar.

As a leader, you can make subtle changes in your organization for employees. During large meetings, instead of coffee, donuts, and sweets, you can have platters of fresh vegetables and fruit with organic dips. People love this. Everyone is trying to stay healthy, and it is hard when someone puts a platter of chocolate covered donuts under your nose. I have also noticed many organizations have a beautiful container of fruit infused drinking water at the lobby or entrance. There are usually cups and a small trash can for disposal. The water can be infused with lemon and lime slices and even oranges.

There are many recipes online to check out. This sends a message of wellness to all who visit and all who work there. Lemon and lime water is great for the body.

When you begin being mindful of what you put into your body, you will begin to enjoy shopping for groceries and planning your meals. It is even more special if you can share it with someone you love. Become present in every moment. Make memories and make time for the important people in your life. The more you eat whole food, the less you will crave junk. Most restaurants even offer healthy choices, and a lot of restaurants make their meals from scratch. These are the places you will learn to love.

Chapter 52 –Kindness

Kindness is free. Kindness makes everyone smile and feel good. Why isn't there more of it being shared? It doesn't have to be a big thing. The other day, I went to an Aldi grocery store. I was searching for a quarter so I could get a grocery cart. I never keep cash on me, but I found a quarter in my husband's car. However, as I was walking across the parking lot, a girl had unloaded her groceries into her car, and she was bringing the cart back. Instead of putting it back and getting her quarter back, she gave me the cart and said, "hey, here, you can use mine". It only saved me a quarter, but it was a very nice gesture from a total stranger. So, as I took the grocery cart and was walking into the store, another girl was walking over to get a cart. I said, "hey, here is a quarter, it isn't much, but that girl gave me her cart, so the least I can do is pay it forward". She smiled and said, "hey, thanks!". We all shared a smile as we went into the store. I even smiled as I paid my $158.00 grocery tab at the checkout. It is just about being nice.

Another example of kindness happened to me while I was driving through Starbucks. I had ordered one of their egg white & roasted red pepper egg bites and a hot tea. When I reached the window to pay, the girl advised, the person before me paid for my order. I was blown away. It was one of the nicest things anyone had done for me in a while. So, I in turn, paid for the car behind me. I took off with my egg bites and never saw the person's face, but it made me feel good about myself. I do not go to Starbucks often, but when I do, I have made this a tradition for myself.

Recently, my husband's niece was talking about a group of her friends getting together for breakfast, once a year, usually around Christmas time, and everyone pitches in for a huge tip for the waitress. This year, after they visited with each other and were leaving, they handed the waitress an envelope. This year, they gave well over $500 to a waitress. I am sure it changed her life. People are struggling, not just for presents for Christmas, but for food, electricity, rent money, etc. The group does it nonchalantly, so it does not attract any attention. If you are one of those people who like to do things quietly, this is a great idea of an act of generosity.

According to the dictionary, kindness is defined as the quality of being friendly, generous, and considerate. Acts of kindness can make the world a happier place to be. It can provide people with feelings of optimism, confidence, happiness, and encouragement. It can also empower people to repeat acts of kindness they themselves have experienced. The feelings are profound. It doesn't matter if you are poor or wealthy, when someone reaches out and does something nice for you, for no reason, you will always remember that moment.

I have only picked up hitchhikers a couple of times over the past fifty years, but one I will never forget. It was snowing heavily in OKC, and I was on I-40 on my way to work. I could barely see the highway in front of me, but I noticed someone walking on the side of the freeway. I pulled over and waited for them to catch up with me. I rolled down the window and I asked if I could give them a ride. The person took off their hat and mask and I saw it was a young girl about fourteen. She had a backpack on. She said, "that would be great, I am trying to make it downtown to the bus station". I told her I could do that.

As she got into the car, she was freezing to death. I didn't want to pry, but I asked her where she was headed. She said she was trying to go home. She had run away from home a couple of years before and she had not talked to her parents since that time. She removed her backpack as she got into the car, and it wasn't until we were about five miles down the road, she opened it up. Inside was a newborn baby. It was naked. All it had was the backpack to keep it warm. My eyes filled up. That morning, I was feeling sorry for myself because I did not have a lot of money to buy Christmas presents for my two sons. I believe God has a way of talking to you in moments like this. Instantly, I was grateful for what I did have: a roof over my head, heat, food, and my kids had warm clothes.

I drove her to the OKC bus station, which is not a safe place. She did not have any money and I used what money I had left in my checking account to buy her a one-way ticket to Kansas. I gave her all the change I had in my purse and my ashtray of the car. It wasn't much. But suddenly, I could not think of a thing I might need it for that was more important that this girl and her baby.

I am not sharing this to get attention. I am sharing this because of how it brought tears to my eyes during a rough time of my life. I have never forgotten this lesson. I say it is a lesson because I feel like a higher power reached down and touched my heart in a way only I could understand, in that moment. Kindness can change a life around. In this instance, you would think it might have changed the young girl's life, but it was mine instead.

Chapter 53 – Integrity

Integrity is about doing the right thing, even when nobody is around. Great leaders are those who walk their talk. Integrity is defined as having strong moral principles, moral uprightness. A person with strong integrity behaves ethically, even behind closed doors.

Traits of Integrity include being gracious, respectful, honest, trustworthy, responsible, helpful, patient, and mature. A person who has an unshakable ethic is a person who is strong with their principles and refuses to change or be coaxed into unethical practices.

Great organizations have great leaders who expect integrity from their employees. They look for this when they hire someone. If you, as a leader, want to have the respect of your people, you must have a solid strong moral code. You must be unshakable. With a world that sometimes looks as if it has gone sideways, it is the leaders who stick to their principles that will turn it back around.

Be one of those leaders. Set the bar high for everyone to follow.

This is a great topic which most organizations already have in their training center. Everyone moans and groans about going to Ethics classes, but it truly is one of the most important stones when building your foundation and building your legacy you want to leave behind.

Chapter 54 – Understanding Change

Mankind has continued to evolve for thousands of years. This is due to constant inventions and ideas along with cultural societies merging around the globe. Technology has increased and advanced at such a rapid rate, it is allowing people all around the world to connect and learn about each other. When this happens, people learn there are more ways to accomplish something than their own idea. It also forces organizations to adapt to new cultures, new technology, new inventions, new competition.

Change is something that happens deep down, inside, and is a process. It is driven by either someone who leads an idea of change or outside circumstances. A manager needs to have a special set of skills to adapt to the tensions that change causes in an organization. The way a manager or leader handles the tensions that arrive from the change will set the tone for the climate and the outcome (Palmer, Dumford & Buchanan, 2017).

It is crucial for a manager to assess the level of change prior to implementing needed changes in an organization.

Assessing the depth of change takes time. A manager must decide whether the change is nothing or minor or if it is a problem that just needs to be fixed because someone never did in the past. This type of change is considered "not on the scale" (Palmer, Dumford & Buchanan, 2017).

Shallow change is making minor adjustments such as cutting costs or fine tuning a piece of equipment to produce better output. Sustaining innovation is looking at the big picture. This might mean new ideas and closing out things that do not work any longer. There might be better products or better ways of doing things. A company might decide to create a new department to oversee the waste or spending in a certain department (Palmer, Dumford & Buchanan, 2017).

Deep change will include looking at an organizations whole mission and goals. The values of a company might change through change of leadership. When this happens, it can move an organization into deep changes that will affect a whole new outlook and vision of where the company is headed and why. Usually, this also creates a new culture for the company to cling to that shifts people's thinking and behavior (Palmer, Dumford & Buchanan, 2017).

Deeper change comes when there is a shift in the way of a company's thinking such as new equipment that might cut expenses because it eliminates the need for people. This might include also new ways of reaching out to customers to do business, such as social media. Keeping up with the times and changes can be difficult especially if a company has been solid for many years without major changes. This could also include embracing diversity in the workplace. With many people arriving to the United States, more and more people are finding jobs in companies that never had a diversified workforce. This requires a lot of changes to take place within human resources and education and training that might not have been in place before that (Palmer, Dumford, & Buchanan, 2017).

Off the scale changes can seem catastrophic. This is when everything is disrupted, and the boundaries of organizations are reconstructed with brand new innovation and brand-new technology that is unknown to everyone. This sometimes creates a panic, especially for old timers who have been with a company for a long time. They can be intimidated by new innovation and new technology. Sometimes, these same experienced and knowledgeable, valuable employees feel forced to retire because the idea of massive changes such as these are too much to cope with.

Many managers will look at change through six different types of views: (1) director, (2) coach, (3) navigator, (4) interpreter, (5) caretaker, and (6) nurturer (Palmer, Dumford & Buchanan, 2019). It is important for managers to assess the changes that are coming or have arrived. They need to know what caused the change, what drives the change and whether the change is caused by external pressures or internal.

Leadership must evaluate the depth of the change and the nature and evaluate all employees and organization to decide the level of readiness for change. An organization needs to understand clearly what is going to change and what needs to change first to be successful (Anand & Barsoux, 2017). There will be managers who step up with a vision that is easy for all to see and follow. The managers who are skilled in change will be the ones who move forward and upward with the new changes.

Organizations need to decide how they are going to share the news and communicate with customers and employees about the changes ahead. They need to be prepared for some to resist and some who will support the new changes. A system must be decided upon that implements the change and allows for adaptability if something does not work as they thought it might.

Involving whole teams in the process of change allows for accountability also. People feel part of something if they can contribute ideas and help set goals. If the process is successful, then the next step is sustainability and forward thinking for the next possible improvement or potential threats that might occur and to have a contingency plan ready.

The many changes that are facing organizations these days include diversity in the workplace, innovation, new technology, global competition, but most of all, creating healthy cultures, healthy organizations, and healthy employees.

Chapter 55 – The Heart & Love

"The heart is the most powerful organ in our body. It sends powerful messages to our body and brain through neurological, hormonal, and electrical signals that not only keep us alive, but can direct our mood and emotions. In fact, it is the strongest source of our bio-electrical energy. It is 40-60% stronger than the electrical energy of the brain" (Howard Martin, 2022). The HeartMath Institute has over thirty-one years of scientific research on the psychophysiology of stress, resilience, and the interactions between the heart and the brain. There are over three hundred and twenty-seven independent studies not connected to this institute but have written periodicals and research papers.

Anxiety, stress, depression, anger, frustration all has a negative effect on our heart rhythm and our emotions. In turn, it come out through our behavior. Likewise, happiness, joy, calmness, care, and love have a positive effect on our heart and mind. In turn, it comes out through our behavior. There are many tools available to teach us how to keep our hearts and mind in optimal state of health. It is worth checking out.

Everyone knows what the heart is capable of. I am not talking about pumping blood throughout your body and to the brain. I am talking about emotions and the power of love. As I spoke a lot about energy in my Part I book, I will mention it once again. Everything is energy. Our bodies are made up of energy. Our heart is energy. It is important, not only as leaders, but as human beings, to keep our instincts sharp, our bodies in tune, and our hearts open to the energy around us. It helps us, help others. It starts with you. If we can become balanced in our lives in all dimensions of wellness, we can become authentic transformational leaders, and lead this global change. A global change of leading from the heart. It is time we serve others, not of others serving us.

Chapter 56 – Recap

Change is hard. I keep saying this because I am always surprised at how big a topic change management really is. People and organizations are naturally resistant to change, especially, if things have flowed fine in the past. In reality, you blink, and you are behind the times, in almost everything. It is so important to keep up with change.

Time is really the only thing we need to manage and manage well. It gets away from all of us and it is something we can never get back. It is so important for organizations to have short term plans and long-term plans. Along with this, a time frame to reach each goal and then another to upgrade or reevaluate, down the road.

Leaders need to be transparent and ensure everyone is on the same mission. The employees and the leaders should all be able to tie their daily work into the organizational goals. Leaders who walk their talk will establish an organization like no other. People respect and will follow people who are transparent, honest, loyal, respectful, have high levels of integrity, make them feel valued, and work at building the best workforce ever. Leaders who work hard at retaining good employees that are valuable to the organization, must know it is worth it. Leaders who also recognize toxic employees, who are not working in the best interests of the organization and are swift in removing the toxicity from the organization, will gain respect from all others.

It is great when leaders lead by example. When leaders encourage employees to participate from all levels, it opens the door for great minds to create not only a better organization, but a better world. Leaders can create training videos with their managers. These can be shared with all new employees. It makes everything more real, more human, and brings everyone together. These videos can be updated every year as new goals and missions are defined. It is also great to get to know your people. Creating a mentoring program within the organization is a terrific idea to share knowledge between employees of all levels. It also builds strong relationships. Leaders who are not afraid to admit they do not know everything, and are open to learning, tears down barriers and fears employees may have when it comes to approaching leadership for help. Learning to be an excellent listener is important at all levels. If something is not working, it is okay to fail. Just keep failing forward. Every person has the capability of making a difference in the lives of others. You just must step out there and speak from the heart.

Leaders who have resilient hearts and lead by example are very inspiring. People come from all walks of life and all kinds of backgrounds. We are all human. Nobody knows everything in the world. We all make mistakes. Being open to learning is the key. Growth is possible for every single person.

Resilience is learning from errors or mistakes and not making those mistakes again. It is also about being an example for others to learn by. Believing in yourself and knowing that no matter what has happened in your life, you deserve this, you deserve better, and know you are meant for more. It is also about not being afraid to say no, more often. Sometimes, we get so bogged down, doing for others, that we forget about ourselves. Staying true to yourself is what matters. Because if you don't take care of yourself, you are no good to anyone else.

I do believe resilience can be promoted, by being resilient yourselves, you will encourage other people to be that way too.

We are entering a new time of leadership. It is the first time in history we have five different generations of people working together. This takes a new mindset. Most people spend at least one third of their life working. The workplace should be stress free, inspiring, and empowering to everyone in the organization. People have enough problems with life, alone, it is important to provide resources for employees in hard times. We all have them. The person you hire is more than what you see. It is important to get to know your people. It is important for you to share who you are and what it important to you. People need transparency, respect, trust, and to be valued.

Unwell people in the workforce cost 2.2 trillion dollars a year. It is important to create a new mindset and put our money where our mouths are. It is time to create employee wellness in the workplace, like no other time in history. It is needed, for leaders. It is needed for employees. It is time to be in the forefront globally, of this new holistic leadership style.

Chapter 57 –Conclusion

As you finish this book, you are probably wondering, where do you begin? It all starts with you. It is crucial you take care of yourself, your whole self. Look at all of the different dimensions of wellness and be honest where you rank with each one. If you have anything out of balance, then do what is necessary to get everything back in alignment. This may take a day. It might take several months. Create the change you need to feel joy in every aspect of your life.

Outline a plan for your organization. It can be a base to start from. Bring your leaders into the mix and share with them, this book. Look at your entire organization. Get everyone involved in this new change. What is toxic? What is healthy? Look at every single person you have working. What plans do you have for that person, for the future? What value do they bring to the table? What are their weaknesses? What are their strengths? Who are they? What kind of career development center or plan do you have in place? What resources can you bring into the organization that will help people be healthy? What resources can you bring into the organization that will inspire every person to want to work for you? What do you need to do to put smiles on every person's face? What do you offer that will draw in top talent from all over? Are you a global organization? How do you rank with expatriates and repatriation programs? Do you have adequate support for these people? Are you a small business owner? Do you do a lot of the work yourself because you are afraid to delegate and trust your employees? If you are, you must be exhausted. It all starts with you.

When we open our hearts and begin working from our true selves, your happiness and joy will flow out of you and into all those around you. People will feel good about coming to work. People will feel good about what they do. They will feel valued, by you, by the organization. The job will become more like a second home. It will be a safe place, filled with support, of all kinds. Leaders will be walking their talk. Leaders will want every single employee to be healthy. Leaders will be empowering. Leaders will be inspiring. Leaders will lead the way into the future with a new holistic mindset of whole wellness.

You need to find a way to encourage and inspire people at all costs. You cannot do this cleanly if you have a pile of unresolved issues of your own. As a leader, it is imperative you deal with your own issues in a healthy way and get them out of the way, so you can grow and be a teacher of excellence to those who follow you. Leaders must have the highest emotional intelligence they can, to move into the future role of holistic leadership. As leaders, it is imperative we keep our instincts sharp, our minds clear, so we can tune in to the people around us. It helps us, help others.

Being centered, calm, at peace, is critical for making better decisions, taking the right roads, and becoming a great leader. Leaders must do whatever it takes to keep their instincts intact. This helps when dealing with crisis issues or employees who are in crisis mode. Leaders who develop routines for themselves to cope with their own stress, are light years ahead of others who do not place their own emotional wellbeing first. When creating holistic wellness programs for your organization, it is exciting when a leader works with employees from the ground up. This is a perfect time to share your own story or to find a way to connect with your people on a human level. You would be surprised how many people fear leadership. Take that fear away. Be real. Be human. Be kind. It is time that leadership serves the people, not the other way around.

In 2019, only three years ago, the cost of unhealthy people at work was a 2.2 trillion-dollar loss in the United States alone.

This was 12% of the GDP. The breakdown of that is as follows: $1,100 billion dollars costs of chronic disease; $250 billion dollars cost of work-related injuries; $300 billion dollars costs of work-related stress; $550 billion dollars cost of disengagement of work. These statistics should grab your attention. Without employees, there would not be an organization. Leaders forget about this. Not only do they forget about it, but they also do not give much thought on how employees drive the success or failure of an organization.

It makes sense for us to do whatever we can to keep our employees healthy and happy. This is not only for employees; it is for leaders also.

Message from the Author

I hope you enjoyed my book. I hope you found some good take a ways that will help you in your career, your organization, or your personal life.

As we move into a more transformational holistic leadership era, I hope the ideas and information I wrote about gives you something to not only think about, but to act upon. People need leadership that makes them feel good about themselves and lets them know that what they do makes a difference.

There will be a global shift in the types of leadership around the world and in every organization. The dictators and aggressive toxic leaders will be a thing of the past. They will be replaced with leaders who serve the people and not the other way around. They will be inspirational, empowering, kind, respectful, strong yet gentle souls, who will want to see their people grow, and become the best they can be. These leaders will be very emotionally strong. They will also put their own wellness as a priority. They will become the best role models ever seen in history.

Change takes time. If you look around, the winds of change have already arrived. It has been a long time coming. Everything comes full circle. If you or your organization are experiencing hard times, stay strong, better days are coming around.

If you have any questions or want to reach out to me, I am available through email. My email address is tholzberlein@gmail.com. Please feel free to drop me a line.

Again, thank you for taking time out of your life to be part of mine for a little while.

Tracy G. Jilge-Holzberlein

References

Alhamami, N. M., Wan Ismail, W. K., Kamarudin, S., & Abdullah, F. Z. (2020). Linking Emotional Intelligence and Transformational Leadership to Job Performance in a Conflict-Stricken Environment. *Talent Development & Excellence, 12*, 2153.

ANAND, N., & BARSOUX, J.-L. (2017). What Everyone Gets Wrong About Change Management. *Harvard Business Review, 95*(6), 78–85. Retrieved from https://search.ebscohost.com/login.aspx?direct=true&db=bth&AN=125760038&site=eds-live&scope=site

Aguinis, H., Gomez-Mejia, L. R., Martin, G. P., & Joo, H. (2018). CEO pay is indeed decoupled from CEO performance: charting a path for the future. *Management Research: The Journal of the IberoAmerican Academy of Management, 16*(1), 117. Retrieved from https://search.ebscohost.com/login.aspx?direct=true&db=edb&AN=129549552&site=eds-live&scope=site

ATAPATTU, S. (2019). From "Our Common Future" to sustainable development goals: Evolution of Sustainable Development Under International Law. *Wisconsin International Law Journal, (36)2, 215-246.*

BACHELDER, C. (2018). *Dare to Serve: How to Drive Superior Results by Serving Others.*
Berrett-Koehler Publishers.

Bao, Y., & Ge, L. (2019). Linking transformational leadership and value congruence among
Chinese police force: The mediating role of goal clarity and the moderating role of public service motivation. *Australian Journal of Public Administration, 78*(3), 373–3

Baque VIllanueva, L. K., Mendoza, M. A., Salcedo, R., & Izquierdo Morán, A. M. (2020). The
Transformational leadership, sustainable key for the development of Ecuadorian companies. A neutrosophic psychology approach. *Neutrosophic Sets & Systems, 34,* 143–152.

Bartram, T., & Dowling, P. J. (2013). An international perspective on human resource management and performance in the health care sector: toward a research agenda. *International Journal of Human Resource Management, 24*(16), 3031–3037. https://doi.org/10.1080/09585192.2013.775024

Beckton, J.B., Walker, H.J. & Jones, F.A. (2014). Generational differences in workplace behavior. *Journal of Applied Social Psychology, 44(3) 175-189*

Bennett, K., & Rhodes, S. C. (1988). Writing Apprehension and Writing Intensity in Business and Industry. Journal of Business Communication, 25(1), 25–39. https://doi.org/10.1177/002194368802500102

Berry, P. (2010). Communication Skills for Women in the World of Corporate Business: Getting It Right and Moving Up! *American Journal of Business Education, 3*(1), 83–90. Retrieved from https://search.ebscohost.com/login.aspxdirect=true&db=eric&AN=EJ1060332&site=eds-live&scope=site

Blackwell, D., Dudney, D., & Farrell, K. (2007). Changes in CEO compensation structure and the impact on firm performance following CEO turnover. *Review of Quantitative*

Finance Accounting, 29(3), 315–338. https://doi.org/10.1007/s11156-007-0034-y

Boudreau, J.W. & Ramstad, P.M. (2005). Talentship, Talent Segmentation, and Sustainability. A new HR decision science paradigm for a new strategy definition. *Human Resource Management, (44)2, 129.*

Boxed in by your inbox: Implications of daily e-mail demands for managers' leadership behaviors. Journal of Applied Psychology, 104(1), 19–33. https://doi.org/10.1037/apl0000343

Brisco, D., Schuler, R. S., & Claus, L. (2009). International human resource management: Policies and practices for multinational enterprises. South Asian Journal of Management 23(2), 154-159.

Broderick, Renae & John W. Boudreau. (1992). Human Resource Management, Information
Technology, and the Competitive Edge. *The Executive, 6*(2), 7.

Building Talent: THE VERY BEST OF 2017. (cover story). (2017). *TD: Talent Development, 71*(10), 24–27. Retrieved from https://search.ebscohost.com/login.aspx?direct=true&db=bth&AN=125614982&site=eds-live&scope=site

Coleman, Isobel. (2010). The Global Glass Ceiling: Why Empowering Women Is Good for Business. Foreign Affairs, 89(3), 13. Retrieved from https://search.ebscohost.com/login.aspx?direct=true&db=edsjsr&AN=edsjsr.25680912&site=eds-live&scope=site

Chaigneau, P., & Sahuguet, N. (2018). The Effect of Monitoring on CEO Compensation in a Matching Equilibrium. *Journal of Financial & Quantitative Analysis, 53*(3), 1297–1339. https://doi.org/10.1017/S0022109017001065

Collyer, F. M., Willis, K. F., & Lewis, S. (2017). Gatekeepers in the healthcare sector: Knowledge and Bourdieu's concept of field. Social Science & Medicine,

186, 96–103. https://doi-org.vlib.excelsior.edu/10.1016/j.socscimed.2017.06.004

Conyon Martin, J. (2018). Comments on two sides of CEO pay injustice: The journal of the Iberoamerican academy of management. *Management Research, 16*(1), 107-116. doi: http://dx.doi.org.vlib.excelsior.edu/10.1108/MRJIAM-11-2017-0791

Crockett, R. O., & McGregor, J. (2007). BUYOUT SHOPS ARE STILL BUYING TALENT. (cover story). *Business Week*, (4057), 044–045. Retrieved from https://search.ebscohost.com/login.aspx?direct=true&db=bth&AN=27240995&site=eds-live&scope=site

Cunningham, C. M., Hazel, M., & Hayes, T. J. (2020). Communication and Leadership 2020: Intersectional, Mindful, and Digital. *Communication Research Trends, 39*(1), 4–31.

Dang, A., Likhar, N., & Alok, U. (2016). Importance of Economic Evaluation in Health Care: An Indian Perspective. Value in Health Regional Issues, 9, 78–83. Retrieved from:

https://doi-org.vlib.excelsior.edu/10.1016/j.vhri.2015.11.00

Davidovitch, N., & Khyhniak, K. (2018). Language Personality in the Conditions of Cross-Cultural Communication: Case-Study Experience. International Education Studies, 11(2), 13–26. Retrieved from https://search.ebscohost.com/login.aspx?direct=true&db=eric&AN=EJ1167626&site=eds-live&scope=site

DeMotta, H. G., Gonzales, S. J., & Lawson, S. (2019). Exploring Strategic Training Approaches that Lead to The Retention of Talented Employees. *Journal of Organizational Psychology*, *19*(3), 48. Retrieved from https://search.ebscohost.com/login.aspxdirect=true&db=edo&AN=138167603&site=eds-live&scope=site

Derousseau, R. (2016). Pondering the Puzzle of IBM. *Fortune, 174*(1), 43–44.

Dimoff, J. K., & Kelloway, E. K. (2019). With a little help from my boss: The impact of workplace mental health training on leader behaviors and employee resource utilization. *Journal of Occupational Health Psychology, 24*(1), 4–19.

https://doi.org/10.1037/ocp0000126

Dordevic, B. (2016). Impact of national culture on international human resource management. Economic Themes 54(2), 281-300.

Eager, H. (2017). Managing mental health in the workplace. *Governance Directions, 69*(3), 142–146

Edwards, S. (2012). Maintaining the Delicate Balance When Developing High-Potential Programs. *T+D, 66*(4), 60–65. Retrieved from https://search.ebscohost.com/login.aspx?direct=true&db=bth&AN=73889011&site=bsi-live&scope=site

Fan, S. X., Cregan, C., Harzing, A., & Köhler, T. (2018). The benefits of being understood: The role of ethnic identity confirmation in knowledge acquisition by expatriates. *Human Resource Management, 57(1),* 327–339. https://doi.org/10.1002/hrm.21839

Farrell, R. Z. (2012). The truth about talent. (Links to an external site.)PM Network, 26(10), 44-47. Retrieved from *http://vlib.excelsior.edu/login?url=http://search.ebscohost.com/login.aspx?direct=true&db=bth&AN=82061827&site=bsi-live&scope=site This article reviews several myths about effective talent management programs and discusses the value that talent management can provide to an organization's bottom line.*

Feinstein, D. (2022). Uses of Energy Psychology Following Catastrophic Events. Review Article, Front. Psychol., 25 April 2022. Sec. Psychology for Clinical Settings. Retrieved from: https://doi.org/10.3389/fpsyg.2022.856209

Finch, D., Hillenbrand, C., O'Reilly, N., & Varella, P. (2015). Psychological contracts and independent sales contractors: an examination of the predictors of contractor-level outcomes. *Journal of Marketing Management, 31*(17–18), 1924–1964. https://doi.org/10.1080/0267257X.2015.1076496

Fröhlich, C., & Gioli, G. (2015). Gender, Conflict, and Global Environmental Change. Peace Review, 27(2), 137–146. https://doi.org/10.1080/10402659.2015.1037609

Gellweiler, C. (2017). Bridging IT requirements to competitive advantage: The concept of IT value planning.

Procedia Computer Science, 121, 145. Configurational Perspective. *MIS Quarterly, 44*(1), 85.

Gundur, R. V. (2019). Using the Internet to Recruit Respondents for Offline Interviews in Criminological Studies. *Urban Affairs Review, 55*(6), 1731–1756. https://doi.org/10.1177/1078087417740430

Habash, T. F. (1999). The impact of audio or videoconferencing and group decision tools on group perception and satisfaction in distributed meetings. The Psychologist-Manager Journal, 3(2), 211–230. https://doi.org/10.1037/h0095872

Haile, S., & White, D. (2019). Expatriate Failure Is a Common Challenge for Multinational
Corporations: Turn Expatriate Failure to Expatriate Success. *International Journal of Business & Public Administration, 16*(1), 27–40.

Hajncl, L., & Vučenović, D. (2020). Effects of Measures of Emotional Intelligence on the
Relationship between Emotional Intelligence and Transformational Leadership. *Psihologijske Teme /*

Psychological Topics, 29(1), 119–134. https://doi.org/10.31820/pt.29.1.7

Hansbrough, T. K., & Schyns, B. (2018). The Appeal of Transformational Leadership. *Journal of Leadership Studies, 12*(3), 19–32. https://doi.org/10.1002/jls.21571

Harter, N. (2015). Introduction-History in the Study of Leadership. *Journal of Leadership Studies, 9*(2), 39–41. https://doi.org/10.1002/jls.21362

Harvard Health Publishing, Harvard Medical School. (2022). Giving Thanks Makes You Happier. Retrieved from www.health.harvard.edu

Hausdorf, P.A. & Robie C. (2018). Understanding subgroup differences with general mental ability tests in employment selection. Exploring sociology-cultural factors across inter-generational groups. *International Journal of Selection and Assessment. 26(2-4), 176- 190*

https://www.doi.org/10.1111/ijsa.12226

Hendron, J. A., Irving, P., & Taylor, B. J. (2014). The emotionally intelligent ministry: why it matters. *Mental Health, Religion & Culture, 17*(5), 470–478. https://doi.org/10.1080/13674676.2013.848424

Heneman, H.G., Judge, T.A., and Kammeyer-Mueller, J.D. (2015). Staffing organizations. (8th Ed). New York: McGraw, Hill/Irwin

Hildebrandt, H. W., & Snyder, R. D. (1981). The Pollyanna Hypothesis in Business Writing: Initial Results, Suggestions for Research. Journal of Business Communication, 18(1), 5–15. https://doi.org/10.1177/002194368101800102

Horst, S.-O., & Järventie-Thesleff, R. (2016). Finding an emergent way through transformational change: a narrative approach to strategy. *Journal of Media Business Studies, 13*(1), 3–21. https://doi.org/10.1080/16522354.2015.1123854

Huang, Q., Jiang, F., Lie, E., & Que, T. (2017). The Effect of Labor Unions on CEO Compensation. *Journal of Financial & Quantitative Analysis, 52*(2), 553–582. https://doi.org/10.1017/S0022109017000072

Hynes, G. E., & Veltsos, J. (2019). Managerial Communication: Strategies and Applications, 7th Edition. Thousand Oaks, CA: Sage.

IBM (2014). Retrieved from http://www.ibm.com/us/en/

IBM. (2020). Website Retrieved from https://www.IBM.com Institute of Integrative Nutrition. (2022) https://www.integrativenutrition.com

Jacobs, B. (2019, December 1). Leading with Gratitude: Eight Leadership Practices for
Extraordinary Business Results. *Booklist, 116*(7), 9.

JAVIDAN, M., BULLOUGH, A., & DIBBLE, R. (2016). Mind the Gap: Gender Differences in Global Leadership Self-Efficacies. Academy of Management Perspectives, 30(1), 59–73. https://doi.org/10.5465/amp.2015.0035

Jiang, Y., & Wang, J. (2018). A Study of Cultural Empathy in Foreign Language Teaching from the Perspective of Cross-cultural Communication. Theory and Practice in Language studies, (12), 1664. Retrieved from https://search.ebscohost.com/login.aspx?direct=true&db=edsglr&AN=edsgcl.566681543&site=eds-live&scope=site

John Hopkins Medicine. (2022). Retrieved from www.hopkinsmedicine.org

Kandogan, Y. (2018). What do managers look for in candidates for international assignments?
Thunderbird International Business Review, 60(6), 823–835. https://doi.org/10.1002/tie.21916

Kang, H., & Shen, J. (2013). International recruitment and selection practices of South Korean
multinationals in China. *International Journal of Human Resource Management, 24*(17), 3325–3342. https://doi.org/10.1080/09585192.2013.770777

Kessler, M.D., D.A. (2012). The End of Overeating, Taking Control of the Insatiable American Appetite

KIDANU, D. (2018). Building talent for the future: Closing the mismatch between skills and demand is crucial as we enter a new, digital era. *International Trade Forum*, (2), 24–25. Retrieved from https://search.ebscohost.com/login.aspx?direct=true&db=bth&AN=132119360&site=eds-live&scope=site

Kifer, Y., Heller, D., Perunovic, W. Q. E., & Galinsky, A. D. (2013). The good life of the powerful: The experience of power and authenticity enhance subjective well-being. *Psychological Science, 24*(1), 280–288.

Kim, H.-E., Kim, H. H., Han, B.-K., Kim, K. H., Han, K., Nam, H., Lee, E. H., & Kim, E.-K.
(2020). Changes in cancer detection and false-positive recall in mammography using artificial intelligence: a retrospective, multi reader study. *The Lancet Digital Health, 2*(3), e138–e148. https://doi.org/10.1016/S2589-7500(20)30003-0

King, K. A., & Vaiman, V. (2019). Enabling effective talent management through a macro-contingent approach: A framework for research and practice. *BRQ Business Research Quarterly, 22*(3), 194–206. https://doi.org/10.1016/j.brq.2019.04.005

Koh, D., Lee, K., & Joshi, K. (2019). Transformational leadership and creativity: A meta-analytic review and identification of an integrated model. *Journal of Organizational Behavior, 40*(6), 625–650. https://doi.org/10.1002/job.2355

Koss, S., & Society for Human Resource Management (U.S.). (2008). *Solving the Compensation Puzzle: Putting Together a Complete Pay and Performance System*. Alexandria, Va: Independent Publishers Group. Retrieved from https://search.ebscohost.com/login.aspx?direct=true&db=nlebk&AN=291642&site=eds-live&scope=site

Kumar, S., Parray, W. M., Khare, S., David, B. E., & Ahirwar, G. (2018). Mental health at the
workplace: A study on non-teaching staff in the university campus. IAHRW International Journal of Social Sciences Review, 6(10), 2014–2016.

Leskowitz, E. (2016). Integrative Medicine for PTSD and TBI: two innovative approaches. Med. Acupunct. 28, 81-183. doi: 10.1089/acu.2016.1168

Lin, S.-H. (Joanna), Scott, B. A., & Matta, F. K. (2019). The Dark Side of Transformational Leader Behaviors for Leaders Themselves: A Conservation of Resources Perspective.

Academy of Management Journal, 62(5), 1556–1582. https://doi.org/10.5465/amj.2016.1255

Majeed, N., Jamshed, S., Nazri, M., & Mustamil, N. M. (2019). Walk the Talk: Bringing Spirituality to Workplace through Transformational Leadership and Emotional Intelligence in Higher Education Institutions. *Jurnal Pengurusan, 56*, 1–19.

Manning, G. & Curtis, K. (2019). *The art of leadership.* (6th ed.). McGraw-Hill.

Martin, Howard. (2022). Engaging the Intelligence of the Heart. Retrieved from: Heartmath Institute. https://www.heartmath.org

Mayo Clinic (2022). Acupuncture Therapy for COVID Related Olfactory Loss. https:::://www.mayo.edu

McGuire, J., Oehmichen, J., Wolff, M., & Hilgers, R. (2019). Do Contracts Make Them Care? The Impact of CEO Compensation Design on Corporate Social Performance. *Journal of Business Ethics, 157*(2), 375–390. https://doi.org/10.1007/s10551-017-3601-8

McNeff, M. E., & Irving, J. A. (2017). Job Satisfaction and the Priority of Valuing People: A Case Study of Servant Leadership Practice in a Network of Family-Owned Companies. *SAGE Open, 7*(1), 1.

Meek, S., Tucker, M. L., Pueschel, A., & Jordan, K. (2019). Introducing Business Communication Students to the Power of Positivity: Providing One Approach. *Journal of Instructional Pedagogies, 22*. Retrieved from https://search.ebscohost.com/login.aspx?direct=true&db=eric&AN=EJ1216822&site=eds-live&scope=site

Miftari, V. (2018). Transformational Leadership Communication in Developing Countries' Business Environment. *Journal of History, Culture & Art Research / Tarih Kültür ve Sanat Arastirmalari Dergisi, 7*(2), 259–264. https://doi.org/10.7596/taksad.v7i2.1436

Morgan, J. F. (2018). Clarifying the Employee/Independent Contractor Distinction: Does the California Supreme Court's Dynamex Decision Do the Job? *Labor Law Journal, 69*(3), 129–140. Retrieved from https://search.ebscohost.com/login.aspx?direct=true&db=bth&AN=131415741&site=eds-live&scope=site

Murphy, H. (2019). Dealing with The Devil: The Triumph and Tragedy of IBM's Business with
The Third Reich. *History Teacher, 53*(1), 171–193.

National Institute of Health. (2022) Recruitment and Early Retention of Women with Advanced Breast Cancer in a Complementary and Alternative Medicine Trial. Retrieved from: www.ncbi.nlm.nih.gov.

Nielsen, P. A., Boye, S., Holten, A., Jacobsen, C. B., & Andersen, L. B. (2019). Are
transformational and transactional types of leadership compatible? A two-wave study of employee motivation. *Public Administration, 97*(2), 413–428. https://doi.org/10.1111/padm.12574

Oliver, S. (2019). Communication and trust: rethinking the way construction industry professionals and software vendors utilize computer communication mediums. Visualization in Engineering, 7(1), N.PAG. Retrieved from https://search.ebscohost.com/login.aspx?direct=true&db=edb&AN=136768667&site=eds-live&scope=site

Palmer, Dunford & Buchanan. (2017). Managing Organizational Change: A Multiple Perspectives Approach, 3rd ed. Chapter 1. New York, New York.

Pasha, M. A., & Ur Rehman, M. Z. (2020). Impact of Transformational Leadership and
Psychological Empowerment on Meaningful Work, Moderating Effect of Organizational Culture. *Abasyn University Journal of Social Sciences, 13*(1), 365–375. https://doi.org/10.34091/AJSS.13.1.26

Passey, D. G., Brown, M. C., Hammerback, K., Harris, J. R., & Hannon, P. A. (2018). Managers' Support for Employee Wellness Programs: An Integrative Review. *American Journal of Health Promotion: AJHP, 32*(8), 1789–1799. https://doi.org/10.1177/0890117118764856

Pavlich, C. A., Rains, S. A., & Segrin, C. (2017). The Nonverbal Bully: Effects of Shouting and Conversational Distance on Bystanders' Perceptions. Communication Reports, 30(3), 129–141.
https://doi.org/10.1080/08934215.2017.1315439

Phillips, C., Bassell, K., Fillmore, L., & Stephenson, W. (2018). Transforming Leaders into
Stewards of Teaching Excellence: Building and Sustaining an Academic Culture through Leadership Immersion. *Contemporary Issues in Education Research, 11*(1), 1–10.

Porter, S., Doucette, N. L., Woodworth, M., Earle, J., & MacNeil, B. (2008). Half the world knows not how the other half lies: Investigation of verbal and non-verbal signs of deception exhibited by criminal offenders and non-offenders. Legal & Criminological Psychology, 13(1), 27–38. https://doi.org/10.1348/135532507X186653

Priatna, D. K., Roswinna, W., & Saputra, J. (2020). Investigation of The Factors Affecting
 Subjective Well Being and Its Impact on Employee Performance in Indonesia: An
Application of Psychosocial Approach. *Talent Development & Excellence, 12*(1), 1112–
1123.

Pulakos, E. D. (2004). Performance management: A road-map for developing, implementing and evaluating performance management systems. Alexandria, VA: SHRM

Foundation. Retrieved from http://www.shrm.org/about/foundation/research/documents/1104pulakos.pdf

Rane, D. B. (2011). Good Listening Skills Make Efficient Business Sense. IUP Journal of Soft Skills, 5(4), 43–51. Retrieved from https://search.ebscohost.com/login.aspx?direct=true&db=bth&AN=78153521&site=eds-live&scope=site

Ruiz, Don Miguel. (1997). The Four Agreements. Https://www.thefouragreements.com

Schultz, C., & Walt, H. van der. (2015). *Reinventing HR: Strategic and Organizational Relevance of the Human Resources Function.* Randburg, South Africa: KR Publishing. Retrieved from https://search.ebscohost.com/login.aspx?direct=true&db=nlebk&AN=1124508&site=eds-live&scope=site

Schuster, W. M. (2018). Artificial Intelligence and Patent Ownership. *Washington & Lee Law Review, 75*(4), 1945–2004.

Schwarz, R. (2022). Association for Comprehensive Energy Psychology. Https://www.energypsch.org

Selected Cross-Cultural Factors in Human Resource Management. (2008). HR Magazine, 53(9), 1–9. Retrieved from https://search.ebscohost.com/login.aspx?direct=true&db=bth&AN=34312815&site=eds-live&scope=site

Shapiro, D. L., White, F., & Shackleton, B. W. (2019). Overcoming the tribe's effect: The overview effect as a means to promote conflict resolution. Peace and Conflict: Journal of Peace Psychology. https://doi.org/10.1037/pac0000414

Soares, A. T. N. (2018). Epistemology, Methods and Theories of Communication in the Big Data Era: A Critical Panorama of Social Media Research. Comunicação e Sociedade, 33, 167–181. https://doi.org/10.17231/comsoc.33(2018).2912

Solinger, O. N., Jansen, P. G. W., & Cornelissen, J. P. (2020). The Emergence of Moral
Leadership. *Academy of Management Review*, *45*(3), 504–527.
https://doi.org/10.5465/amr.2016.0263

Stapleton, P. (2019). The Science Behind Tapping. Carlsbad: Hay House Inc.

Strycharczyk, D., & Elvin, C. (2014). *Developing Resilient Organizations: How to Create an Adaptive, High-Performance and Engaged Organization.* London: Kogan Page. Retrieved from https://search.ebscohost.com/login.aspx?direct=true&db=nlebk&AN=816420&site=eds-live&scope=site

Subotnik, R. F. (2015). Psychosocial Strength Training: The Missing Piece in Talent Development. *Gifted Child Today, 38*(1), 41–48. Retrieved from https://search.ebscohost.com/login.aspxdirect=true&db=eric&AN=EJ1050192&site=eds-live&scope=site

Sundström, A. (2019). Exploring Performance-Related Pay as an Anti-corruption Tool. *Studies in Comparative International Development, 54*(1), 1–18. https://doi.org/10.1007/s12116-017-9251-0

Thite, M., Budhwar, P., & Wilkinson, A. (2014). Global HR Roles and Factors Influencing Their Development: Evidence from Emerging Indian IT Services Multinationals. *Human Resource Management*, *53*(6), 921–946. https://doi.org/10.1002/hrm.21621

Thomason, S. J., Brownlee, A., Beekman Harris, A., & Rustogi, H. (2018). Forced distribution systems and attracting top talent. *International Journal of Productivity & Performance Management*, *67*(7), 1171–1191. https://doi.org/10.1108/IJPPM-06-2017-0141

Thomson, R. A., Overall, N. C., Cameron, L. D., & Low, R. S. T. (2018). Perceived regard, expressive suppression during conflict, and conflict resolution. Journal of Family Psychology, 32(6), 722–732. https://doi.org/10.1037/fam0000429.supp

TODT, K. (2015). A Venture of Her Own: Early American Women in Business. *Early Modern Women: An Interdisciplinary Journal*, *10*(1), 152–163. https://doi.org/10.1353/emw.2015.0012

Tripathy, M. (2018). Assertiveness – A Win-Win Approach to Business Communication. *IUP Journal of Soft Skills, 12*(2), 48–56. Retrieved from https://search.ebscohost.com/login.aspx?direct=true&db=bth&AN=130776569&site=eds-live&scope=site

Tooma, M., & Beech, N. (2016). Improving wellness in the workplace: Think holistically and
Beyond. *Governance Directions, 68*(8), 497–499.

Turban, E., Pollard, C., & Wood, G. (2017). *Information Technology for Management* (11 ed.):
Hoboken, New Jersey: John Wiley & Sons.

Ugwu, F. O., Idike, A. N., Ibiam, O. E., Akwara, F. A., & Okorie, C. O. (2020). Transformational leadership and management safety practices: Their role in the relationship between work pressure and compliance with safety work behavior in a health-care sector industry. *Journal of Psychology in Africa, 30*(1), 1–8. https://doi.org/10.1080/14330237.2020.1716551

Ulutürk, B., & Tayfun, R. (2019). The Roles of Transformational Leadership, Communication
Competence and Communication Satisfaction on Employees' Job Satisfaction. *Journal of Communication Theory & Research / Iletisim Kuram ve Arastirma Dergisi, 49*, 48–68.

Uzuegbu, C. P., & Nnadozie, C. O. (2015). Henry Fayol's 14 Principles of Management: Implications for Libraries and Information Centres. *Journal of Information Science Theory & Practice (JIStaP)*, 3(2), 58–72. https://doi.org/10.1633/JISTaP.2015.3.2.5

Valine, Y. A. (2018). Why cultures fail: The power and risk of Groupthink. *Journal of Risk Management in Financial Institutions*, *11*(4), 301–307. Retrieved from https://search.ebscohost.com/login.aspxdirect=true&db=bth&AN=133397495&site=eds-live&scope=site

VERBONCU, I., & ZEININGER, L. (2015). The Manager and the Managerial Tools: Job Description. *Review of International Comparative Management / Revista de Management Comparat International*, *16*(5), 603–614. Retrieved from https://search.ebscohost.com/login.aspxdirect=true&db=bth&AN=115183772&site=eds-live&scope=site

Volkema, R. J., & Niederman, F. (1996). Planning and Managing Organizational Meetings: An Empirical Analysis of Written and Oral Communications. Journal of Business

Communication, 33(3), 275–296. https://doi.org/10.1177/002194369603300304

Webster, N. A. (2017). Rural-to-rural translocal practices: Thai women entrepreneurs in the Swedish countryside. *Journal of Rural Studies, 56,* 219–228. https://doi.org/10.1016/j.jrurstud.2017.09.016

Wood, E. (2015, April 1). Bachelder, Cheryl. Dare to Serve: How to Drive Superior Results by
Serving Others. *Library Journal, 140*(6), 100.

World Health Organization. (2020). Working for better health for everyone, everywhere. Retrieved From https://www.who.int/

YoungKi Park, & Mithas, S. (2020). Organized Complexity of Digital Business Strategy: A

Yuan-Duen Lee, Pi-Ching Chen, & Chin-Lai Su. (2020). The Evolution of the Leadership
Theories and the Analysis of New Research Trends. *International Journal of*
Organizational Innovation, 12(3), 88–104.

Zaidi, U. (2020). Health and Rehabilitation Science specialties, physical activity, and dimensions of wellness among the students of PNU. *Heliyon, 6*(1). https://doi.org/10.1016/j.heliyon.2020.e03204

Zheng, C. (2016). *International Human Resource Management: Trends, Practices and Future Directions*. Nova Science Publishers, Inc.

About the Author

Tracy G. Jilge-Holzberlein is a wife, mother, and Nana T to four grandchildren, and an entrepreneur who believes in personal development. She holds an MBA in healthcare administration from Excelsior University, New York. She is a certified International Health Coach through the Institute of Integrative Nutrition program based out of New York. She was certified in 1988 by the Oklahoma State Supreme Court as a Certified Mediator. Although she did not continue the mediation path as a career, the skills she learned have served her well.

She comes from very humble beginnings, which she shares in this book. She has dreams of living off the grid with her husband, being self-sufficient while growing her own food, making gourmet goat cheese, writing, and pursuing her art through inspirational acrylic and oil paintings, and opening her own global wellness center, where Eastern Medicine meets Western Medicine.

She is forward thinking in terms of balancing sustainable alternative energy with the oil and gas industry, and inspiring positive social change in executive leadership. She is a firm believer of our nation being completely self-sufficient and safe, while finding ways to support issues such as global warming and immigration. She believes we are obligated to leave a healthy legacy for generations to follow.

Tracy has real life experiences, from walking away from expected norms, to following her dreams of traveling north to Alaska. She is the great granddaughter of Ethel Nelson, the first woman to work for the Alaskan Railroad. She loves gold panning, rock hounding, and making jewelry. She is inspired by strong women of all cultures who are not afraid of taking the road less traveled. She has more than forty years of work experience combined, including public service through criminal justice industry, healthcare industry, private industry, customer service industry, restaurant industry, government employment, and entrepreneurship.

Tracy enjoys traveling and spending time with her family. She resides in Norman, Oklahoma.

www.ingramcontent.com/pod-product-compliance
Lightning Source LLC
Chambersburg PA
CBHW052341220526
45465CB00003BA/899